Learning
Networking

Ramesh Bangia
B.Sc., Dip. Comp. Sc.
Formerly: Managing Editor, Software Today
Formerly: Incharge Computer Centre, Hindustan Copper Ltd., New Delhi

KHANNA BOOK PUBLISHING CO. PVT. LTD.

Learning Networking— Ramesh Bangia

Published by: **Khanna Book Publishing Co. (P) Ltd.**
Regd Office: 1694-95, Nai Sarak Delhi-110006
Telephone: 011-23256658, 23283211
Fax: 011-23256658
E-mail: contact@khannaedu.com
Website: www.khannaedu.com

ISBN 81-87522-00-3

Typeset at

MAYANK CONSULTANTS
65/80 Rohtak Road, New Delhi 110 005
Tel.: 571 5968, 572 7854

Printed and Bound by Narain Printers and Binders, Delhi.

PREFACE

Learning of a software is both easy and difficult. It depends upto what level you are planning to learn. If you are learning only for the working use, then it is very easy. But, when you try to go deep into it, then you realise how difficult it is to master it.

Networking is such a vast subject that it will take a lot of time to understand it fully. This book has been written in mind to make you aware of the options available in the software and how they can be used. It is like telling the child about the steps and stairs. You are the one who is to climb the stair. This book will just guide you how to use the stairs.

I am indeed debited to my publishers Khanna Book Publishing Co. Pvt. Ltd., specially Vivek and Puneet for their suggestions and encouragement given in producing this book.

I would like to thank my family specially my wife Sadhna, kids Mayank and Samarth, for without their criticism this book would not have seen the day.

Suggestions for improvement of the book are indeed welcome.

Ramesh Bangia

CONTENTS

1

Introduction to Networking

Introduction

Networking is a concept, where 2 or more than 2 computers are joined together to share information. This can be in the form of data or programs. These computers can be within a walking distance or in the same building of the office or in the same city or even across the cities.

But, why is this needed. Have you ever found yourself rushing from one computer to another in your office or home, attending to several different jobs at various locations? Or do you often find yourself moving files that need printing form a PC that you happen to be working on the PC that is connected to the printer? All of these situations can be made easier by allowing the various machines to communicate with each other – by networking the PCs.

The distance between the computers is narrowed down by the telephone lines. The information from the computer is converted to the media understandable by the communication lines and then transferred from one place to another.

With networking you can not only share data and programs, but can also share the resources like printers, scanners, etc. In PC technology, such a collection of computers, all located within a few thousand feet of each other, is called Local Area Networking.

Networking Basics

Networking several computers together allows data to be transmitted form one machine to another in rapid and easily managed data streams. This sharing of data allows many of the resources that are located on a single machine to effectively become available to all other machines on the network.

These resources can be physically located on the machine, e.g., as files on the hard disk, or connected logically to the machine. An example of a logically connected resource would be a printer that is connected to a PC, but which is then available over the network to other machines on that network.

An alternative situation would be where access to the Internet is available to all the PCs on a network through a special communication device attached to the network. Access to all external and internal resources are thus made available to PC users on the network.

A network server provides network services to a user workstation (server) on the network. Services can range from sharing database and files, printers; communications or other network resources. Thus, the network servers are also called file servers, print servers, communication servers, etc. They can be dedicated to the task of providing network services.

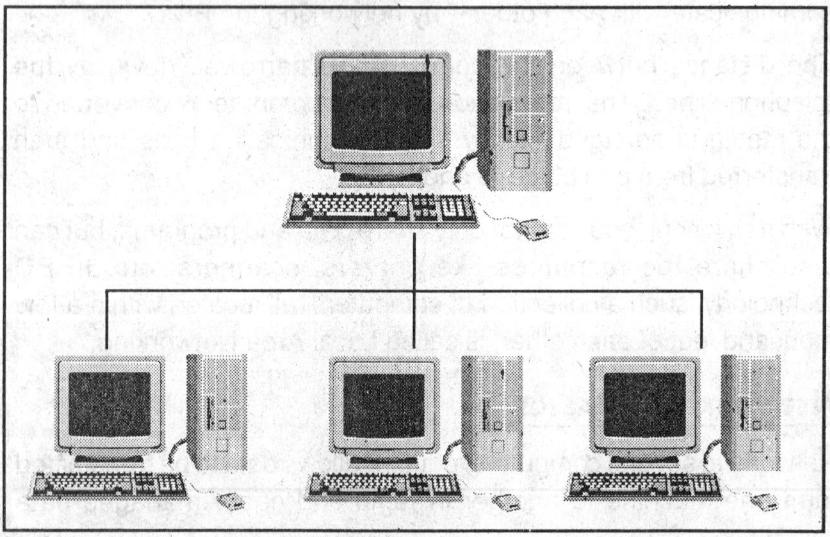

They are then called dedicated network servers. Otherwise, they may be called non dedicated servers. A typical networking is shown on the last page.

Another factor which also favours the networking is the cost factor.

Cost Reduction

If you have 2-3 computers attached in a single networking system, you may go in for a single printer which can be used by all of them. The same goes for other devices like Scanner, Plotter, etc. This results in lots of costs.

The main advantages of Networking can be clubbed as follows:

Resource Sharing

There are two main types of networking systems. The type used for larger networks is known as the Client/Server model. This model involves using a powerful computer that runs a Network Operating System and acts as the 'server'. The Network Operating System then runs the server, supplying network services to the other 'client' computers.

These services might include the management of file transfers, running printing jobs, or even running applications across the network. For example, a word processing software package running on a PC is actually being 'served' form the server across the network, rather than being loaded onto the PC's local hard disk.

The problem with the Client/Server model is that it requires specialised hardware, software and to a large extent skilled networking techniques to configure and maintain the network. All of this can become expensive.

The second model, the Peer-to Peer system or resource Sharing is fortunately a lot easier to implement and maintain and it is this model that we will use in this book.

Resource Sharing is incorporated into Windows 98 and allows all network users access to all resources such as the hard drives, directories, printers or CD-ROM drives that are available on the network. It also allows access to external resources across the network via special intermediary devices.

Resource Sharing involved each computer on the network taking on equal an equal part in the networking process and is ideally suited to smaller networks.

SECURITY

Being able to have complete access to all resources on the network is not always desirable. It is often the case that certain resources may need to be restricted to certain users.

Resources Sharing within Windows allows for this and incorporates the ability to protect access to particular resources with passwords. These passwords can then be stored within the windows 98 configuration files so that access to protected resources is automatically assigned once the user has gained access to the network; the relevant passwords is therefore only entered once during the network login procedure. This function can also be disabled so that a password is required every single time the user attempts to access a protected resource.

Password access can also be configured to allow the user to read but not to change a particular resource or to allow full access, including the ability to write to a resource (which would be necessary for sending jobs to a printer).

Each individual resource can also be configured separately so that different passwords and access rights can be assigned for different resources

TYPES OF NETWORKING

The three basic types of networks are:

1. Local Area Networks or LAN

2. Metropolitan Area Network or MAN
3. Wide Area Network or WAN

Let us see them in details.

Local Area Network

A local area network (LAN) is two or more computers directly linked within a small well-defined area such as a room, building, or group of closely placed buildings. A LAN may be made up of only microcomputers or any combination of microcomputers and large systems.

A LAN usually consists of the following:

1. Two or more computers
2. Peripheral devices such as printers and hard-disk drives
3. Software to control the operation of the computers or other devices connected to the LAN
4. Special cables, usually coaxial or fibre optic, to connect the computers and other devices
5. A plug-in board to handle the data transmissions.

Some computers require that all the computers be of a certain brand, while others allow a variety of brands to be connected. The number of computers in a LAN varies from smaller LANs that typically connect 2 to 25 computers, to large LANs that can connect as many as 10,000 computers.

The length of the cable connecting a computer to a LAN also varies depending on the LAN. Most LANs allow cables of about 1,000 feet, but some allow cables of several miles to be used. The data transfer speeds range from several thousand bits per second to around 10 million bits per second. The programs that control the LANs also vary in the features they offer. Some programs allow the user of more than on operating system; others allow only one. On some

LANs file access is limited to one user at a time; on others, more than one user can access a file simultaneously.

Hardware for LAN

The following are the major hardware components/devices for establishing LAN:

1. Transmission Channel
2. Network Interface Unit or NIU
3. Servers
4. Workstations

Transmission Channel for LAN

Generally four types of channels are used for data transmission in a LAN. These are:

1. Twisted Pair Cables
2. Coaxial Cables
3. Fibre Optic Cables
4. Radio Waves

About these you will read in a next chapter.

Interface for LAN

Network interface units connect each devices in the LAN network to shared transmission device. It contain the rules or logic to access the LAN. NIU is also used to implement LAN protocols and for device attachments. Its function depends on the type of topologies (to be told later in the this chapter), used in LAN.

Server and Workstations

One of the major benefits of implementation of LAN is sharing expensive resources such as storage devices, printers, etc. This is achieved through providing servers on the LAN. It is dedicated computer that controls one or more resources. This contains both hardware and software interface for LAN. Three major categories of services used in LANs are:

1. File Server
2. Printer Server
3. Modem Server

In networking, file server is used to share storage for files. Besides providing storage space for files in a LAN environment, it is used for taking periodical backup, and also to provide gateway to other servers with and between LANs. Similarly printer server is used to handle printing works of all workstation connected in the network. In LAN environment also modem is required to get connected to other network or simply to use a telephone. A modem server is used to share this expensive resource by all connected workstations in a network ring.

Software for LAN

LAN operating system is required to operate on the LAN system. It has basically two aspects:

1. Server Software
2. Workstation Software

LAN operating system facilitates :

1. Sharing of expensive resources, e.g., printer, storage space, etc.
2. Security for data
3. Connection to other network

There are various types of LAN operating system. Some popular LAN operating systems are :

— Novel Netware

— Ethernet

— Corvus

— ArcNet

— LAN Server

— Omni Net

— PC Net

— IBM PC LAN

— Etherlink Plus, etc.

Wide Area Networks or WAN

A wide area network is two or more computers that are geographically dispersed, linked by communication facilities such as telephone system or microwave relays. This type of network is usually limited to use by large corporations and government agencies because of the high cost involved in building and maintaining them. A WAN is a network that links separate geographical locations and this network can be a public system or any of the various packet switched services provided by the public telecommunication agencies.

The main difference between a WAN and LAN is under the complete control of the owner, whereas the WAN needs the involvement of another authority like telecom department. LANs are successful and capable of handling very high data transfer rates at low cost because of the small area covered. Besides LANs have a lower error rate than WANs.

Transmission Channel for WAN

Generally 3 types of channels are used for data transmission in a WAN. These are:

1. Radio Waves
2. Micro Waves

3. Communication Satellites

Hardware Requirements for WAN

There are mainly 4 hardware devices which are required to establish linkage between geographically separated computers. These are:

1. Bridges
2. Routers
3. Gateways
4. X.25 Standard Interface

These are explained below.

Bridges

These are used to connect two LANs that use the identical protocols over a wide area. The bridge acts as an address filter which picks up packets from one LAN that are intended for a destination on another LAN and passes these packets on the network. The amount of processing required at the bridge is minimal because all the devices use the same protocols. In case the distance between two LANs is very large then the user is required to employ two identical bridges at either end of the communication link.

Routers

It is a special type of device that can be used to connect networks that may not be similar. Such type of devices provide connectivity between two LANs and two WANs over large geographical distances. These devices operate at the Network Layer of the OSI model. These devices participate in a routing protocol to access the network topology, and on the basis of this information routers compute the best route from a sender to the receiver.

Gateways

These are used to connect two dissimilar LANs. The terms Gateways and Routers are used interchangeably, though there is discriminating difference between the two. A router operates at the network layer whereas a gateway operates on the application layer of the OSI model. A gateway is required to convert data packets from one protocol format to another before forwarding it, as it connects two dissimilar networks.

X.25 Standard Interface

X.25 is a protocol for interfacing to a Public Packet Switched Network. It is not a protocol used for implementing a network. Two systems that support X.25 can't necessarily be connected back-to-back. They can only be connected through a DCE in a Public Packet Switched. International Telegraph and Telephone Consultative Committee (ITTCC) developed X.25 as the standard interface between the Data Terminal Equipment (DTE) and Data Circuit Terminating Equipment (DCTE). This recommendation has been widely accepted as the industry standard for public packet switched networks.

Types of Wide Area Networks

There are mainly two types of WAN:

Public Networks

These are those networks which are installed and run by the telecommunication authorities and are made available to any organization or individual who go for their subscription.

Private Networks

The basic technique used in all forms of private WAN is to use private circuits to link the locations to be served by the network. Between these fixed points the owner of the network has complete freedom to use the circuits in any way they want. They can use the circuits to carry large quantities of data or for high speed transmissions. Private wide area networks can be built using whatever standard technology is available.

Topology

There are ways in which you can connect the various computers for networking. This physical arrangement is called Topology. Different types of topologies are:

The Ring Topology

As the name suggests all the server/nodes are joined together to form a ring. There is no central server in this case. A ring may be unidirectional or bi-directional. A unidirectional ring moves data in one direction only; a bi-directional ring moves data in both directions, but only one direction at a time. In a unidirectional ring, if one computer breaks down, special software is required to keep the network functional. When one node malfunction in a bi-directional ring, a message can usually be sent in the opposite direction still allowing the node to communicate with all the other active nodes in the network.

Advantages of the Ring Network

1. **Short cable length:** the amount of cabling involved in a ring

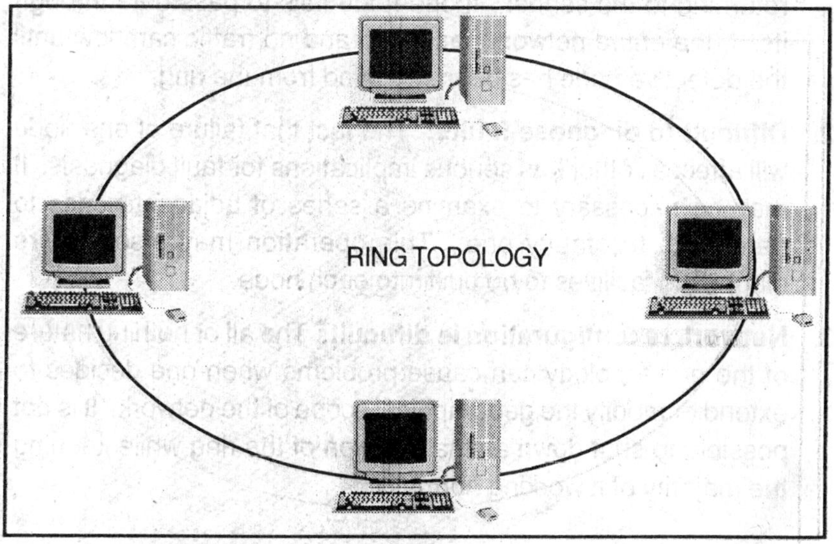

topology is comparable to that of a bus and is small relative to that of a star. This means that less connections will be needed, which will in turn increase network reliability.

2. **No wiring closet space required:** Since there is only one cable connecting each node to its immediate neighbours, it is not necessary to allocate space in the building for wiring closets.

3. **Suitable for optical fibers:** Optical fibers offer the possibility of very high speed transmission. Because traffic on a ring travels in one direction, it is easy to use optical fibers as a medium of transmission. Also, since a ring is made up of nodes connected by short segments of transmission medium, there is a possibility of mixing the types used for different parts of the network. Thus, a manufacturing company's network could use copper cables in the office area and optical fibers in the factory areas, where electrical interference may be a problem.

Disadvantages of the Ring Network

1. **Node failure causes network failure:** the transmission of data on a ring goes through every connected node on the ring before returning to the sender. If one node fails to pass data through itself, the entire network has failed and no traffic can flow until the defective node has been removed from the ring.

2. **Difficult to diagnose faults:** The fact that failure of one node will affect all other has serious implications for fault diagnosis. It may be necessary to examine a series of adjacent nodes to determine the faulty one. This operation may also require diagnostic facilities to be built into each node.

3. **Network reconfiguration is difficult:** The all or nothing nature of the ring topology can cause problems when one decides to extend or modify the geographical scope of the network. It is not possible to shut down a small section of the ring while keeping the majority of it working normally.

4. **Topology affects the access protocol:** Each node on a ring has a responsibility to pass on data that it receives. This means that the access protocol must take this into account. Before a node can transmit its own data, it must ensure that the medium is available for use.

The Bus Topology

In this case all the server/nodes share a common bus of connecting cables. Every computer can communicate directly with every other computer or device in the network. Each node is given an address. To access a particular, a user just needs to know its address. This topology is frequently used with local area networks. Going through a hierarchy of nodes is not necessary.

Advantages of the Bus Network

1. **Short cable length and simple wiring layout:** Because there is a single common data path connecting all nodes, the bus topology allows a very short cable length to be used. This decreases the installation cost and also leads to a simple, easy to maintain, wiring layout.
2. **Resilient architecture:** The bus architecture has an inherent simplicity that makes it very reliable from a hardware point of view. There is a single cable through which all data passes and to which all nodes are connected.
3. **East to extend:** Additional nodes can be connected to an existing bus network at any point along its length. More extensive additions can be achieved by adding extra segments connected by a type of signal amplifier known as a repeater.

Disadvantages of the Bus Network

1. **Fault diagnosis is difficult:** Although the simplicity of the bus topology means that there is very little that can go wrong, fault detention is not a simple matter. In most LANs based on a bus, control of the network is not centralized in any particular node.

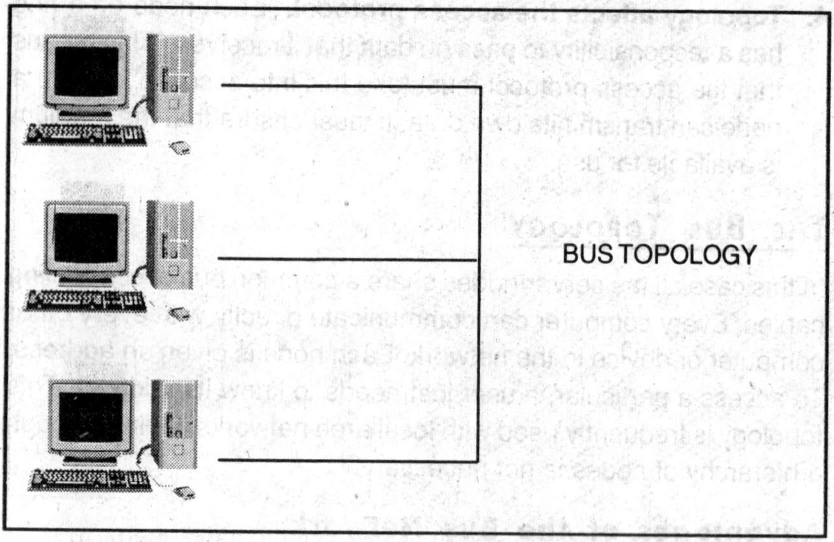

This means that detection of a fault may be performed from many points in the network.

2. **Fault isolation is difficult:** In the star topology, a defective node can easily be isolated from the network by removing its connection at the center. If a node is faulty on a bus, it must be rectified at the point where the node is connected to the network. Once the fault has been located the node can simply be removed. In the case where the fault is the network medium itself, an entire segment of the bus must be disconnected.

3. **Repeater configuration:** When a bus-type network has its backbone extended using repeaters, reconfiguration may be necessary. This may involve tailoring cable lengths, adjusting terminators, etc.

4. **Nodes must be intelligent:** Each node on the network is directly connected to the central bus. This means that some way of deciding who can use the network at any given time must be performed in each node. It tends to increase the cost of the nodes irrespective of whether this is performed in hardware of software

The Star Topology

In this case all the computers and the main server form a star like shape. All the computers are connected to a single main host. All communication first goes through the centralized computer allowing it to control the operation, work load, and resource allocation of the other computers in the network.

For example, a bank with branch offices would typically use a star network to control and coordinate those branches. The advantage is relative simplicity, but a problem exists with the single-point vulnerability of the network. If the central computer breaks down, none of the other computers can communicate with each other.

Advantages of the Star Network

1. **Ease of service:** The star topology has a number of concentration points, i.e. at the central node or at intermediate wiring closets. These provide easy access for service of reconfiguration of the network.
2. **One device per connection:** Connection points in any network are inherently prone to failure. In the star topology, failure of a

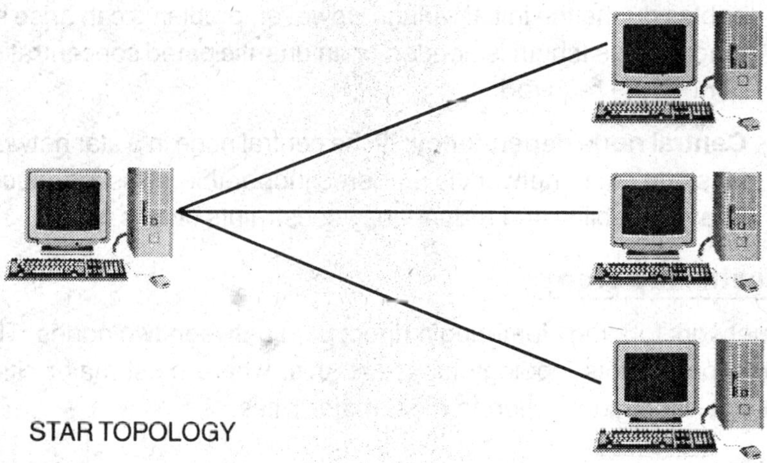

STAR TOPOLOGY

single connection typically involves disconnecting one node from an otherwise fully functional network.

3. **Centralized control/ problem diagnosis:** The fact that the central node is connected directly to every other node in the network means that faults are easily detected and isolated. It is a simple matter to disconnect failing nodes from the system.

4. **Simple access protocols:** Any given connection is a star network involves only the central node and one peripheral node. In this situation, contention for who has control of the medium for transmission purposes is easily solved. Thus in a star network, access protocols are very simple.

Disadvantages of the Star Network

1. **Long cable length:** Because each node is directly connected to the center, the star topology necessitates a large quantity of cable. While the cost of the cable is often small, congestion in cable ducts and maintenance and installation problems can increase costs considerably.

2. **Difficult to expand:** The addition of a new node to a star network involves a connection all the way to the central node. Expansion is usually catered for by providing large numbers of redundant cables during the initial wiring. However, problems can arise if a longer cable length is needed or an unanticipated concentration of nodes is required.

3. **Central node dependency:** If the central node in a star network fails, the entire network is rendered inoperable. This introduces heavy reliability and redundancy constraints on this node.

Mesh Topology

A network topology featuring a direct path between two nodes. The backbone of this topology looks like this, where most major cities have a direct connection to most major cities.

Advantages and Disadvantages of the Mesh Network

- **Units affected by media failure:** Mesh topologies resist media failure better than other topologies. Implementations that include more than two devices will always have multiple paths to send signals from one device to another. If one path fails, the transmission signals can be routed around the failed link. Theoretically, no units are affected by media failure. However, if all paths normally use the maximum capacity of each link, some performance degradation will occur are signals are routed around a failed link.

- **Ease of installation:** Mesh networks are relatively difficult to install because each device must be linked directly to all other devices. As the number of devices increases, the difficulty of installation increases geometrically.

- **Ease of troubleshooting:** Mesh topologies are easy to troubleshoot because each medium link is independent of all

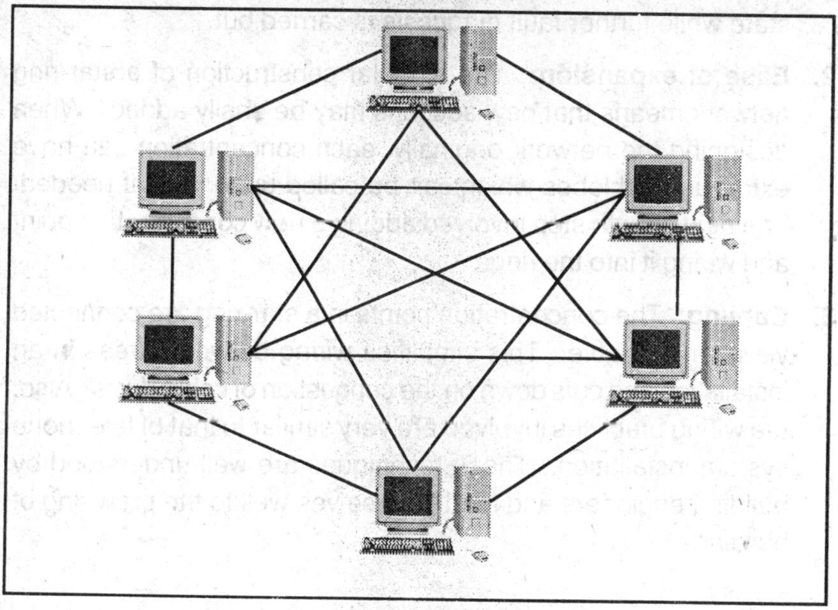

others. You can easily identify faults and can isolate the affected link.

Ease of reconfiguration: Mesh topologies are difficult to reconfigure for the same reasons that they are difficult to install.

Hybrid Topology

A combination of two or more network topologies. The resultant is a hybrid network. Although the backbone is mostly a mesh network, each local loop is a star network with the central office at each hub.

Advantages of the Hybrid Network

1. **Fault diagnoses and isolation:** The presence of concentration points in the network greatly eases fault diagnosis. If a fault is detected on the network, the initial problems to find out which concentration point in the ring is to blame. The fact that this ring is quite small in relation to the total size of the network makes this problem more manageable. The offending concentration point can be isolated easily, leaving the network in a fully functional state while further fault diagnosis is carried out.
2. **Ease of expansion:** The modular construction of a star-ring network means that new sections may be easily added. When designing the network originally, each concentration can have extra, unused lobes which can be called upon later, if needed. The next growth step involved adding a new concentration point and wiring it into the ring.
3. **Cabling:** The concentration points in a star-ring are connected via a single cable. This simplifies wiring between areas in an installation and cuts down on the congestion of cable ducts. Also, the wiring practices involved are very similar to that of telephone system installation. These techniques are well understood by building engineers and lend themselves well to the prewiring of buildings.

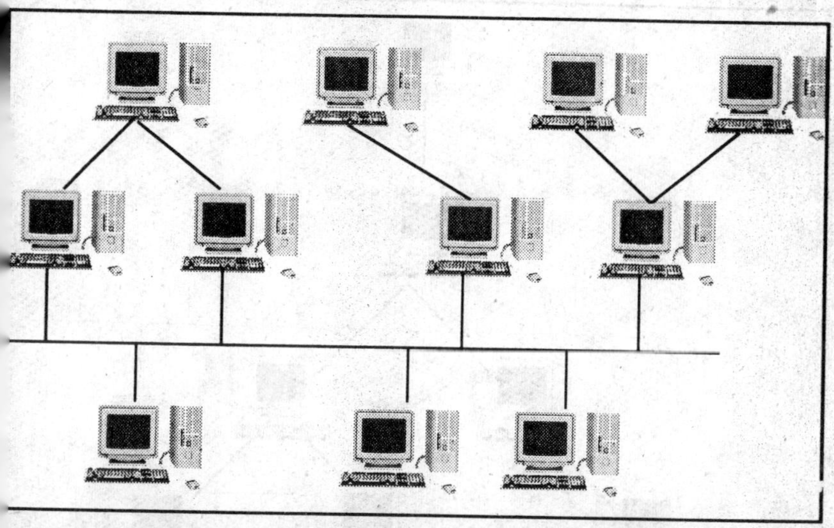

Disadvantages of the Hybrid Network

- **Intelligent concentration points required:** Depending on the implementation used, the concentration points may need to have built in intelligence/processing ability. This will be necessary if it is to assist in network fault diagnosis, node isolation or conversion from one form of transmission medium to another.
- **Cabling:** The intercloset cabling in a star ring is critical to its operation. This may mean that redundant cabling in the form of one or more back up rings may be necessary to meet reliability requirements. The largest section of the network (i.e. between the concentration points and the nodes) is laid out in a star. This means that a considerable amount of cable may be required.

ree Topology

rom a purely topological viewpoint, this network resembles a terconnection of star networks. Individual peripheral nodes must ansmit to and receive from one other node only, toward a central ode. An advantage of a tree structure is that functional groupings an be created.

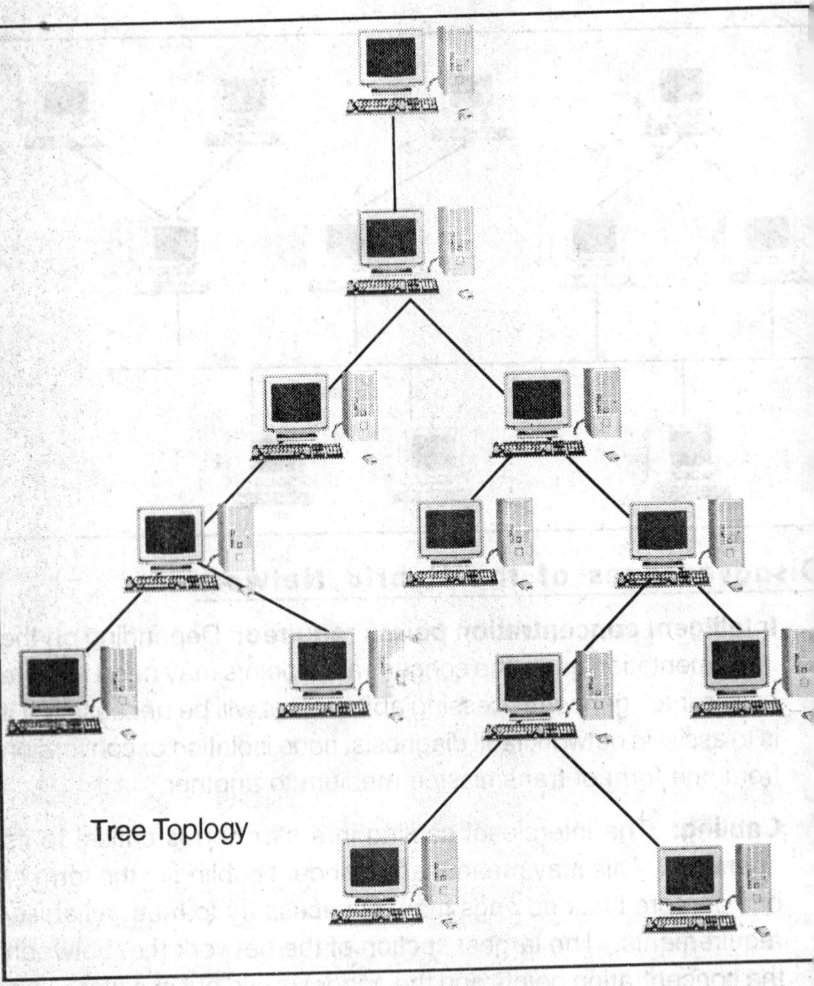

For example, one branch could contain all the general ledge terminals, another branch all the accounts receivable terminals, an so on. If one branch stops functioning, the other branches in a tre network are not affected. However, data movement through thi network can be slow.

Advantages of the Tree Network

1. **Easy to extend:** Because the tree is of its very nature, divide into subunits, it is easier to add new nodes or branches to it.

2. **Fault isolation:** It is possible to disconnect whole branches of the network from the main structure. This makes it easier to isolate a defective node.

Disadvantages of the Tree Network

1. **Dependant on the root:** If the "headend" device fails to operate, the entire network is rendered inoperable. In this respect, the tree suffers from the same reliability problems as the star.

APPLICATIONS OF NETWORKING

In business, government organizations, universities and many other organizations networks of all types of computers provide tremendous benefits. Four of the most compelling benefits are as follows:

SIMULTANEOUS ACCESS

In business computing, most office workers use the same software package. With a network, business can save a lot by purchasing special network versions of the most commonly used software rather than buying separate copies for each machine. When employees need to use the software, they simply load it from a shared storage device into their own desktop computer.

Since a single network copy of the software can serve the needs of large number of users simultaneously, all the employees also save the storage space that the software program would occupy on his computer's disk drive. The same is true of data that multiple employees need access to at the same time. Another major area of computer network advantage is access to remote databases.

SHARED PERIPHERAL DEVICES

The best incentive for small businesses from computers networking is sharing of peripheral devices, especially expensive ones such as laser printer and scanners.

Easier Backup

In business, data can be extremely valuable, so making sure that employees backup their data is critical. One way to address this problem is to keep all valuable data on a shared storage device that employees access through a network. That way, one person can be charged with making regular backup of the data on the shared storage device.

Electronic Mail

Computer networking has helped in increasing the speed of the message transfer tremendously. With the help of e-mail, messages can be transferred through computer network within a short span of time. User can send written message without worrying about whether the other user is currently using his/her computer or not. Over centralized networks, the message is delivered almost instantaneously. E-mail cross time zones, can reach many people with the same message, reduces the paper flood and does not interrupt meetings the way a ringing phone does.

Voice Mail

It releases workers from the tyranny of the telephone. In it, if the person being called does not answer, the called is given instructions to dictate a message to the system. The voice mail computer system stores the message in the recipient's Voice mailbox. Later when the recipient dials the mailbox, the system delivers the message. A voice mail system translates the word of a message into digital impulses, which it then stores on disk, just as any other data. Later this message is reconverted to audio form.

The Ethernet Protocol

Ethernet is the most popular protocol used for LAN communications. In essence it uses a digital 'packet' that can contain any other digital information.

Every computer that uses this protocol contains an Ethernet Network Interface Card (NIC) that has a unique address code embedded into a microchip on the NIC. This address is used by the protocol to identify each individual computer. This allows every electronic packet that is sent from one machine to another to contain the destination address for which the packet is intended.

Every computer on the network 'listens' for packets that contain its own address. When a packet is placed on a network, that packet is broadcast to and received by every other computer on the network but only the computer which corresponds to the destination address is allowed to claim that packet and receive the digital information contained within it.

Only a single packet is allowed onto the network at any one time, but the process operates at such a high speed that effectively the packet is delivered to the destination within milliseconds, allowing the next packet access to the network almost immediately.

The Ethernet protocol also provides a means of preventing two computers from trying to place packets onto the network at the same time. When a NIC tries to place a packet onto the network, it first 'listens' to see if there is already a packet being transmitted to and from other machines, If so, then it is forced to wait for a random amount of time (milliseconds), before trying again. This continues until a 'gap' is found and then the packet can be successfully transmitted onto the network.

The Ethernet protocol provides a means of delivering data from any PC on the network to any other on the same network at a theoretical rate of up to 10 Mega bits per second. Ethernet can also be used to connect remotely located PCs, but this requires special communications links to be set up over specialised equipment.

Fast Ethernet

It is a new standard of the Ethernet protocol, based on the existing 10 Mhz standard, but designed to operate at the much faster data rate of 100 Mhz. Mhz stands for megahertz or a million cycles per second and represents the operating frequency of the protocol. The terms 'Mhz' and 'Mega bits per second' are often used interchangeably, but this is only true where one cycle represents one bit (a bit being a unit of data). For many protocols, this direct relationship holds true, but it is not always the case and so the terms should be used with caution.

The TCP/IP Protocol

TCP/IP is actually two protocols. These two protocols are almost invariably use together, hence the term TCP/IP has come to be accepted as describing a single system. We will be using this assumption here.

TCP/IP is the networks protocol that is used throughout the Internet. It was originally developed in American academic institutions as a means of communicating between university computer systems, first locally and then nationally across America and internationally between universities, that formed the basis of what is now know as the Internet.

It is the capability for being used over existing telephone systems that gives TCP/IP (and hence the Internet) its enormous potential for worldwide data communication. Ethernet is designed to run over relatively short distances at a very high data rate, but the physical limitations of the public phone systems mean that this high data rate cannot normally be sustained, except perhaps over the larger truck routes between countries and major cities. TCP/IP however is independent of the various data rates associated with different communication media and so can be used over both very slow and very high speed systems.

Like Ethernet, the TCP/IP protocol uses an addressing system to determine the intended destinations for a data packet, but unlike Ethernet TCP/IP also includes a source address in the data packet. This system of addresses is used to route the data packet across the Internet, very much like the address on a envelope is used to route a letter across the various national postal systems.

However, unlike Ethernet, each packet is not broadcast cross the entire network, but is routed individually using the addressing system to a single destination. This system is known as 'packet switching'.

Packet Switching

When one computer communicates with another using the TCP/IP protocol, it breaks the information it needs to send into 'chunks' small enough for the TCP/IP packet to be handle and then attaches a destination address and a source address. The packet is then sent out across the Internet, containing all of the information it needs to navigate its way to a remote destination.

It is a feature of the Internet that each individual packet can then take one of many different routes via the thousands of intermediate computer systems across the world to reach its final destination. Each computer along the way reads the destination address of he packet and routes it according to certain sets of rules to the next computer system on the Internet.

This fragmenting of information and use of many alternative routes means that the receiving computer may well receive the packets in a different order to that in which they were sent. It must therefore have some means of making sure that it reads the incoming packets in the correct order.

The job of the 'TCP' part of TCP/IP is to ensure that each packet reaches its destination intact and that the packets are numbered effectively so that the receiving computer can put the incoming packets back into the correct order. It is the 'IP' part TCP/IP that looks after the addressing.

Because TCP/IP packets contain a source address as well as a destination address, the receiving computer system also has a way or replying automatically to the sender by simply reading the source address and then generating another TCP/IP packet using this source address as the destination address for the new packet.

Another feature that is very useful part of the TCP/IP protocol is that because each packet is essentially self-sufficient in its journey across the Internet, many packets from different sources can share a single communication channel, allowing perhaps hundreds of thousands of channels to share a single cable at the same time.

2

SETTING UP THE CABLES

INTRODUCTION

So far we have theoretically learned about the networking and how the computers are connected to each other in different type of networkings. In this chapter you will read about the various types of cables used in connecting the computers. We would also look at the various type of conduits and wall boxes used in networking.

First thing first, let us understand about the type of cables that are used for networking.

ETHERNET CABLES

Ethernet cables use RJ-45 plugs. If you have never seen an RJ-45 plug, it looks like a modular phone plug with eight connectors instead of the 4 connectors that phone wires use. The recipe for making cables is:

1. Category 5 Unshielded Twisted Pair (UTP) cable, available at computer stores and electrical supply houses.
2. RJ-45 ends, which are also available at computer and electrical supply houses.
3. An RJ-45 Terminating Tool. This is a tool that enables you to put the RJ-45 ends of the UTP cable. Typically, good terminating tools will work for both 8-wire and 4-wire plugs. They are expensive but they are worth it if you are working on lots of cables.
4. Inexpensive cable continuity tester.

Start with the cable. Strip the outer insulation back about an inch, very carefully, you do not want to damage the wires inside. Notice that you have 4 pairs of wire inside, one is white/orange and orange, one is white/green and green, one is white/blue and blue, and one is white brown and brown.

Separate the wires so that they line up in the following order from left to right.

1. white/orange
2. orange
3. white/green
4. blue
5. white/blue
6. green
7. white/brown
8. brown

Trim the ends so that they are of the same length. This can be done with wire cutters if you have got them, or you can use the cutter edge on your terminating tool.

Now comes the tricky part, insert all 8 wires into the RJ-45 end so that they are inserted as far as possible. Then push the cable jacket up under the notch in the end.

Carefully insert the end in the terminating tool to its full depth and squeeze the terminating tool tight. This will crimp the end onto the cable and connect the pins on the RJ-45 jack to the wires in the cable.

Now do the other end.

You have just made a cable to the 568B cabling spec, the most common wiring used for networking.

If you have followed the instructions, you should be able to plug the cable you have made into a cable continuity tester and see that pin 1 at one end connects to pin 1 at the other end, all the way to pin 8. Do not get discouraged if your first able does not work. Like anything else, this takes practice.

Crossover Cables

If you have got Ethernet hubs or switches to interconnect, it is necessary in many cases to use a specially made cable a crossover cable. Essentially, it looks like a standard 10BASE-T patch cable except that it is wired differently. Most 10BASE-T and 100BASE-T patch cords are straight-through, which means that the colours are lined up the same at both ends.

In a crossover cable, the difference is that the wire on pin 1 at each end must connect to pin 2 at the other end, and pin 3 on each end must terminate at pin 6 at the other end. So the wiring scheme is as follows:

Pin #	*End 1 colour*	*End 2 colour*
1	white/orange	orange
2	orange	white/orange
3	white/green	green
4	blue	blue
5	white/blue	white/blue
6	green	white/green
7	white/brown	white/brown
8	brown	brown

This works because Ethernet only uses pins 1, 2, 3, and 6. A crossover cable connects pin 1 at one end to pin 2 at the other, and pin 3 to 6. It is useful and it is easy to make.

Thinnet Cables

It uses a special kind of coax cable. It is referred to by the coax cabling standards as type RG58 C/U. The main characteristics of this cable are an impedance rating of 50 ohms and an outside diameter of 4.95mm. Various cable manufacturers refer to this cable generically as Thinnet, Thin Ethernet of Cheapernet coax and the specific characteristics may very slightly from vendor to vendor.

Most will guarantee the cable to conform to the Ethernet standard which is technically referred to as the IEEE 802.3 standard.

Advantages & Disadvantages of Thinnet Cables

Advantages:

- Inexpensive

Disadvantages:

- 10MHz Ethernet only
- More vulnerable to network failure

Twisted Pair (UTP)

It is made up of copper. Data cabling systems are now based around the Twisted Pair model. This type of cables are available as two types, referred to as Category 3 (Cat3) UTP and Category 5 (Cat5) UTP where the 'UTP' standing for Unshielded Twisted Pair. Both types consist of eight copper cores arranged as four pairs twisted together and surrounded by a protective sheath.

The twisting of the pairs is carefully controlled during the manufacturing process to give the high speed data carrying capacities associated with this kind of cable. The Cat 3 cable is rated to carry up to 10MHz and the Cat 5 to 100 MHz. As most new installations need to be 'future proofed' for new data technologies, the Cat 5 cable is generally the most popular and as such is more widely available at little additional cost.

Advantages & Disadvantages of Twisted Cables

Twisted Pair 'Star' System

Advantages:

- More compliant to International Standards
- 10 MHz and 100 MHz Ethernet capability
- Less vulnerable to network failure

Disadvantages:

- Requires a distribution hub
- More cabling required

Twisted Pair (STP)

It is also available as Shielded Twisted Pair or STP. This type of cable contains an additional metal shield around the four pairs and is used in installations where protection from excessive electrical noise is required, e.g., in heavy engineering establishments. In most cases this type of additional protection is unnecessary.

Installing Conduits & Wall Boxes

If your working environment does not already contain an easily accessible cable ducting system you may choose to use wall mounted conduits and wall boxes when installing your cabling system. It is well worth considering this, even though it will require extra expense and work, as this will protect your cabling system from damage. This is especially important for the Thinnet system. However, the multiple cables associated with the Twisted Pair system are also likely to require containment to prevent tangles of additional cables from cluttering up your working environment. It is worth nothing here that both types of network topology can be accommodated by similar conduit systems, with just a few minor differences between the two.

Conduits

Plastic conduits with adhesive backings can be used and these are available from most builders, merchants as either 16 mm by 16 mm or 16 mm by 25 mm. The smaller is suitable for Thinnet installations and the later for Twisted Pair. The larger dimensions may be necessary for the Twisted Pair arrangement as multiple cables may be routed through the conduits as opposed to the single cable need for the coax bus.

Wall Boxes

The wall boxes consist of two parts: the backbox (which attaches to the wall) and the faceplate (which fits onto the front of the backbox). The backbox should be the standard 87 mm by 87mm type used for many kinds of wall outlets. Thinnet installations should use backboxes that are 44mm deep, whereas the Twisted Pair connectors can be accommodated in backboxes 37 mm deep.

Faceplates

These are of a specialised type depending on which type of network system is being installed. Faceplates are available either as 'fixed' where the connector adapter is fixed directly into the faceplate or 'modular' where the adapter is retained in a small mounting plate which then snaps into the faceplate. The modular arrangement allows different types of adapters to be combined at a single outlet, e.g., to combine a network outlet module with a telephone outlet module.

Installing the conduit system is simply a matter of deciding the best routers for your cabling system and then cutting your conduits to the appropriate lengths and fixing to the wall or to whatever surfaces are available. The conduits should be routed to your chosen wallbox locations, which are ideally positioned at about 30mm from the floor. If you have a raised floor or a ceiling void that is easily accessible, then you might consider laying your cables loose in these and then routing your conduits directly up or down to the wallboxes, drilling suitable holes in the floor or ceiling.

In all cases, be careful to avoid running your data cabling parallel to any existing power or lighting cables within about 50cm. Crossing the paths of these existing power cables can be safely done provided the data cable crosses the power cable at right angles. Running active data cables in parallel to cables can lead to induced currents, with a consequent degrading or failure of your network performance.

It is not recommended that you attach conduits to furniture, as it is likely that these will be moved at some point, thereby causing potential damage to the cabling system.

Thinnet Cables Installation Design

A coax network installation simply requires that the Thinnet coax cable runs from the PC to the next using the bus topology model.

The cable is typically installed in a conduit that runs around the walls of a room or office suite, with outlet wall points strategically located. At the outlets, the coax cable is routed out of a wall box to a PC and then back again to the wall box via the two wallbox adapter connectors on the wallbox faceplate. This arrangement maintains the bus topology.

it is technically feasible for the coax cabling to run loose from one PC to the next without the need for installing conduits or wall boxes. If you prefer to adopt this method, care must be taken not to damage or disturb the loose cables during the life of the network.

The coax cable connects to each PC via a specialised adapter called a 'T Piece' adapter which taps into the coax bus in a 'T' junction arrangement. This T junction arrangement is used at every PC, leaving the cable ends effectively loose at each end of the bus. These ends must be terminated using a specialised adapter which contains a 50 Ohm resistor. The termination adapters can either be fitted to the rear of the end faceplate adapters, or to the end T Pieces.

Distance Rules

The Thinnet system is defined by an Ethernet cabling standard that requires that certain distance and configuration rules are applied when designing and installing the cabling structure. These rules are as follows:

- A single coax bus is referred to as a segment. Each segment must not exceed 180 meters in length, including the combined lengths of all the coax cables to and from the individual PCs.
- The distance between each T piece adapter on the bus must not be less than 0.5 metre.
- There must be on more than 30 PCs attached to a single segment.

Other Considerations

When designing and installing a coax cabling system, care must be taken to ensure that the cable does not bend excessively or kink at all. The ability of any coax cable to perform to its specifications will be severely affected by excessive bending and especially by kinking. A maximum bend radius is usually quoted for a particular type of coax cable and for Thinnet cable this is usually about 20 mm.

Cabling

Having designed the physical layout of your Thinnet system and installed any conduits and wallboxes, you are now ready to install, terminate and test the cabling.

What You Will Need

You will nee the following before you begin:

- One Thinnet faceplate for each wallbox outlet. These will contain two Thinnet 'barrel' adapters.
- Thinnet coax cable sufficient to connect all of your PCs together in their planned physically locations. Allow approximately one meter of additional coax cable per wallbox outlet to allow an excess for the termination procedure. Don't forget to include

enough cable for the 'flyleads' from the wallbox to the PC and back.

- Two Thinnet Terminator adapters; one for each end of the coax bus.
- One Thinnet T Piece adapter for each PC that you will be connecting to the network.
- Six Thinnet connectors for each PC on the network. That's four for connecting into and out of the Wallbox BNC adapters and two for connecting to the T Piece adapters. If you are not using wallbox outlets then you will only need two Thinnet connectors for each PC, to connect to the T Piece adapter. Whichever way you decide to cable your system, it will probably be wise to purchase some spare Thinnet connectors, as mistakes during the termination procedure are quite likely before you get the hang of it!
- A BNC Crimp Tool, suitable for crimping the Thinnet connectors.
- A pair of cable cutters or pliers for cutting the cable.
- A sharp knife, for cutting and trimming the coax sleeving.
- A small hand-held Multimeter, for testing the continuity and resistance of the finished cabling system.

As an alternative to the sharp knife, a Coax Wire Stripper tool is available that cuts the coax cable sleeving automatically in exactly the right places and to the correct depth.

If you are going to be doing many Thinnet terminations, then the slightly tricky setting up procedure for this tool may well be worth the effort!

Laying the Cable

Once you have acquired the necessary components for the cable installations, begin by laying the coax loosely into the conduits, allowing approximately 50cm of cable to loop out of the walboxes.

Once the cable is in the conduits, you can fit the conduit coverings as you will not need further access except for at the far ends of the cable bus, where the cable should be left loose inside the conduit ready to be terminated.

Terminating the Cable

The cable should now be terminated so that it will connect to the backs of the wallbox faceplate adapters.

First cut the loop as it emerges form the wallbox in the centre using the pilers, leaving two loose cable ends of approximately 25cm. If you are using the automatic Coax Wire Stripper tool then prepare the cable ends according to the tooling instructions for RG58 coax cable type.

If you are not using the Coax Wife Stripper tool, then prepare the cable ends as follows;

1. Cut the cable back to allow enough length from the wallbox to enable you to manipulate the cable for termination, but not so long that the remaining cable length after termination will not fit comfortably inside the wallbox without excessive bending or kinking. This would normally to be about between 10-15 cms from where the cable enters the wallbox from the conduit.
2. If you have been supplied with plastic or rubber cable support pieces, then thread this over the cable now. Then thread the crimp sleeve along the cable. Do this now as it may be difficult to thread it over after removing the outer cable sleeving.
3. Trim the outer jacket to 17mm from the end of the cable using the knife. Be careful not to damage the metal braiding directly underneath the outer sleeving. This can usually be accomplished by cutting lightly around the outer sleeving and then by working the sleeving off, tearing the remaining plastic in the process.
4. Gently loosen the braiding so that it can be folded back over the cable, exposing the second plastic sleeving. You can ease this

process by passing a sharp point forwards through the braiding to loosen the weave. If there is a metal foil around the second plastic sleeving, then gently run a blade around the foil just forward from where the braiding folds back and remove.

5. Trim the inner sleeving back to 5 mm from the end of the cable, again taking care not to damage the copper core beneath. This will expose either a solid copper core, or a series of copper filaments, depending on the brand of cable that you have used. If you have copper filaments, twist them gently together. This is a very important step as it will ensure that stray filaments are not left loose to cause a short circuit after inserting this section into the central pin.

6. Insert the central core into the pin and crimp using the smaller indentations in the crimping tool. If you find that the twisted core will not fit into the pin, then gently untwist the filaments, carefully remove two or three filaments with the cable cutters, re-twist and insert back into the pin.

7. Push the connector body over the pin and cable assembly so that the pin produces a distinct 'click' as it locates correctly within the connector body. Try gently pulling the pin and cable assembly back out of the connector body. If you can do this easily then the pin has not located properly, possibly due to the core bending slightly behind the pin. If this is the case then re-insert and then firmly pull the pin from the front of the connector body using a pair of nose pilers, being careful not to damage the pin. You could use a piece of cloth between the pin and the jaws of the pilers to do this. Improper location of the pin is a common cause of poor network performance.

8. Fold the braiding filaments back over the connector body so that they lie neatly and evenly around the outside of the knurled collar at the back of the connector body. If necessary, trim the filaments back so that they sit against the collar and end a few millimeters from the main connector body.

9. Slide the crimp sleeve forwards and over the braiding until it butts against the back of the connector body. The braiding will now be trapped between the knurled collar and the crimp sleeve. Now crimp the crimp sleeve the larger identification on the crimp tool (ensure that the crimp sleeve stays butted against the back of the connector body during the crimp operation).

Any cable support can now be slide forward over the crimp sleeve to complete the termination process. Having completed the first termination, repeat the process for all the wallbox rear connections and for the far ends of the cable bus.

When all of the terminations are complete, add the Terminator Adapters to both ends of the cable and plug in all of the terminated wallbox connectors into the rear of the Thinnet faceplates. Ensure that the connected faceplates will mount comfortably onto the wallboxes without undue bending or kinking of the coax cable behind the faceplates, but do not screw into place yet, leaving the faceplates loose for the time being.

Coax Flyleads

Now cut two lengths of coax cable for each PC, sufficient to reach from the wallbox to the back of the PC and allowing for any routing around furniture, etc. Remember that these cable lengths are the most vulnerable to potential damage from users and route them so that the possibilities of damage are minimised. Do not, of course, run cables across walkways, etc, where they will present a 'trip' hazard.

For each PC, connect both flyleads to the 'straight through' part of the T Piece adapter and then connect the other ends of the flyleads into Thinnet faceplate at the wallbox.

You should now have a complete coax bus, with Thinnet Terminator adapters at each end and the coax cable bus running in and out of the wallboxes from one T Piece adapter to the next.

Testing the Coax Bus

Testing the coax bus is a relatively simple matter of checking the electrical continuity of the bus circuit using a small Multimeter. This is best done by checking the T Piece adapters for the combined electrical effect of the presence of both Terminator Adapters at either end of the coax bus. Any breaks or shorts in the circuit will then show up as an incorrect reading.

Firstly, ensure that your bus is complete, with all wallbox, T Piece and Terminator adapter connections in place. Set up your Multimeter to read up to 50 Ohms. Then read the resistance between the exposed central pin and the connector body of any of the T Piece adapters on the bus.

If this reading is between 20 and 30 Ohms, then congratulations! – your coax bus cabling system is complete and functional. It should ideally ready about 25 Ohms, this being the combined result of the two 50 Ohm resistors within the Terminator adapters, arranged 'in series'.

If not, then there is either a shorted or broken circuit somewhere along the length of the bus. If the resistance reading is close to zero Ohms, this indicates a short; if the reading is close to infinity, this would indicate a break in the circuit.

Test for the location of a fault as follows:

1. Start at left-hand end of the bus. Remove the Terminator adapter and using the Multimeter set up as before, check for a reading of approximately 50 Ohms resistance between the central pin and the body of the Terminator adapter. If this is correct, then reconnect the Terminator adapter and move to the first wallbox along the bus. Otherwise you will need to replace the Terminator adapter.
2. Disconnect the left-hand connector from the rear of the wallbox faceplate and check the resistance across this connector. If the left-hand connector produces the correct reading, then this section of the bus so far is functional and the problem must

therefore lie further along the bus. If not, then the fault lies between the left-hand Terminator adapter and this connector. As the fault is unlikely to be within the cable itself, then one of the two connectors between here and the left-hand Terminator adapter is likely to be t he cause of the fault. As there is no way to test exactly which of the two is causing the problem, you will need to reterminate the one and test and then the other if this does not solve the problem.

3. Having established that the bus is functional to this point and that any further faults must lie further along the bus reconnect the left-hand connector to the rear of the wallbox faceplate. Then disconnect the right-hand connector from the rear of the wallbox faceplate and test both sides in the same way as before. If the reading to the left-hand side is now incorrect then the fault lies along the flylead section external to the faceplate. You can then isolate which particular section is responsible by testing to the left at the T Piece.

You can see that this is a process of moving along the bus to each wallbox in turn, then breaking the bus and testing backwards to check for continuity to the left-hand Terminator adapter at each point, correcting any errors that appear as you go. Continue this process until both sides of the bus produce the correct resistance, or until you reach the right-hand Terminator adapter. Finally, test this for 50 Ohms resistance. When you are satisfied that any faults have been corrected, reconnecting he entire bus will produce a combined resistance of 25 Ohms at the T Piece.

Twisted Pair Installation – Design

A twisted pair network is based around a central distribution hub. The function of the Ethernet hub is to receive incoming Ethernet packets from a PC and then to broadcast these unchanged to all other PCs on the network. The hub is often referred to as a repeater hub, because of the process of receiving ethernet packets and then replaying or 'repeating' them to several other PCs.

All of the network PCs are connected to the hub via individual twisted pair cables to ports on the hub device. The main advantage of this arrangement is that a fault in any single cable or PC interface on the network can be detected at the hub and automatically isolated from the rest of the network. This ability to 'intelligently' isolate faults is a common feature of most Ethernet hubs.

There are various types of Ethernet hubs available but for the moment we will simply treat the hub as a device with several ports. The cabling simply consists of running individual twisted pair cables from each PC to a port on the hub. This can either be done directly, or by running the cabling through a conduit system to strategically located wallboxes and then via a 'flylead' to the PC.

The connection to both the PC interface and to the hub is via a standard connector commonly known as the RJ45 Modular plug. The adapter socket used at the wallbox is similar to the one used at the ports on the hub and is commonly known as an RJ45 Outlet Module, or a Cat 5 Outlet Module to denote compliance to the more modern 100Mhz standards. In designing the twisted pair cabling system we will assume compliance to the Cat 5 standard, and Unshielded Twisted Pair (UTP) cabling.

Distance Rules

When designing a Twisted Pair cabling system, certain distance limitations must be considered. These limitations are due to electrical standards requirements that must be met when the ethernet hubs are designed, and simply state that the end-to-end distance between hub and the PC interface must not exceed 100 meters. This is further modified to take account of the use of flyleads and wallbox interfaces, etc., such that in this instance the total length of the flylead must not exceed 5 metres, with the remaining 95 metres allowed for the main cable.

Twisted Pair Installation – Cabling

Having designed the physical layout of your Twisted Pair system and installed any conduits and wallboxes you are now ready to install terminate and test the cabling.

What You Will Need

You will need the following before you begin:

- One Cat 5 RJ45 faceplate for each wallbox outlet. These will contain one or two Cat 5 RJ45 Outlet Modules in either a fixed or modular arrangement.
- Two or three 'stuffer caps', for punching down the twisted pair cores at the punch down blocks on the Outlet Modules.
- Cat 5 UTP cable sufficient to connect the hub to all of the PCs in their planned physical locations. Allow approximately 50cm of additional cable per RJ45 outlet to provide an excess for the termination procedure. Don't forget to include enough cable for the 'fluload' from the walbox to the PC.
- Three RJ45 Modular Plugs for each PC on the network. That's two for the flylead and one for connecting to the Ethernet hub. If you are not using wallbox outlets then you will only need two RJ45 plugs to connect the hub directly to the PC. It will probably by wise to purchase some spare RJ45 Modular Plugs, as mistakes during the termination procedure are quite likely!
- An RJ45 Termination Tool.
- A pair of small cable cutters or pliers for cutting the cable.
- A sharp knife, for cutting and trimming the UTP sleeving.
- A small hand-held Multimeter, for testing the continuity of the finished cabling system.

Hub Location

The hub can be located in any convenient position that has access to a power point. It is common for the hub to be kept somewhere secure to avoid any accidental disconnection or tampering.

If the total span of the network exceeds 100 metres, then it would be sensible to locate the hub somewhere near the middle of the system to prevent the cabling distance rules being broken.

Laying the Cable

Once you have acquired the necessary components for the cable installation, being by laying the UTP cable loosely into the conduit. Allow approximately 25cm of cable to extend out of the wallboxes for termination and enough cable to reach to the hub location at the other end. Once the cable is in the conduits, you can fit the conduit coverings as you should not need further access to the cable within.

Terminating the Cable

The UTP cable contains 8 copper cores, arranged in four pairs an colour coded according to an international standard. This color coding is used to ensure correct termination at the RJ45 Modular Plug and at the rear of the RJ45 Outlet Module.

As you lay each cable between the hub and the wallbox outlet, mark the cable at both ends with a sequential numbering system using tape, or a market pen. This will allow you to identify which cable goes to which wallbox.

Terminating the Outlet Module

Terminating the UTP cable onto the cat 5 Outlet Module is done by 'punching down' the cable cores into 'punchdown blocks' on the Outlet Module. Terminate the UTP cable (to the RJ45 Outlet Module) at the wallbox as follows:

1. Cut back the UTP cable to about 15cm from the point where it enters the wallbox cavity, using the cable cutters.
2. Trim the outer jacket to 50mm form the end of the cable using the knife. Be very careful not to damage the insulation of the individual cores directly underneath the outer sleeving.

   As you lay each cable between the hub and the wallbox outlet, mark the cable at both ends with a sequential numbering system using tape, or a market pen. This will allow you to identify which cable goes to which wallbox.

This can usually be accomplished by cutting lightly to a depth of about 1 mm around the outer sleeving and then by working the sleeving off, tearing the remaining plastic in the process.

You will find that the cores the color and arranged in pairs as follows:

- Green/White and White/Green
- Orange/White and White/Orange
- Blue/White and White/Blue
- Brown/White and White/Brown

You will also find that the 'punchdown block' on the Outlet Module is color coded in a similar way.

Beware: There are many different types of RJ 45 Outlet Module available, but all with identical functions. The main difference is that some require a specialised and relatively expensive 'punchdown' tool, while others supply some form of stuffer cap.

3. Arrange the twisted pairs so that the green and down pairs lie to the left and the blue and orange pairs lie to the fight at 90 degrees to the cable. The cable is then placed in the gap between the two punchdown blocks, so that the twisted pairs lie in the gap between the punchdown blocks and the front section of the module.
4. Untwisted each pair a couple of turns and guide each individual core into its respective slot according to the color coding. Take care not to untwist the pairs by more than about 15mm from the termination slot. Untwisting a pair by more than this can affect network performance at high speeds.
5. The stuffer cap is then pushed over the top of the punchdown block and forced down until the cores appear at the limit of the

slots in the stuffer cap. If you are feeling strong, placing the Outlet Module on a hard surface and pushing down firmly with the thumb should provide enough 'punchdown' force. Otherwise, tap lightly down with a track hammer, or use a pair of slip pliers. If you cannot obtain Stuffer Caps, then an 'Insertion Tool' will serve the same purpose.

6. Excess cores in the gap between the punchdown blocks can then be removed by carefully running a sharp blade along the insidc lcdgc on thc punchdown block, taking care not to damage the cable.

Terminating the Modular Plug

Terminating UTP cable with an RJ45 Modular Plug requires the use of a specialised termination tool.

You will need to terminate the cables that will connect to the hub, as well as the flyleads that will connect the wallbox outlet to the PC. If you are using ready-made flyleads then the latter will not be necessary.

Terminate the Modular Plugs as follows:

1. If you have been provided with a Strain Relief boot for your plug, then feed this onto the cable first.
2. Trim the outer jacket to 20mm from the end of the cable using the knife. Be very careful not to damage the insulation of the individual cores directly underneath the outer sleeving.
3. Untwist the pairs and arrange the cores. Arrange the cores so that they lie as flat as possible and in as straight a line as possible.
4. Use a sharp blade or the cable cutters to accurately trim the cores at a right angle to the cable to 13mm from the cable sleeving.
5. Check the order of the color coding. Then, hold the RJ45 Modular Plug in your right hand so that the metal contacts are facing towards you and the rear of the plug is to the left and hold the cable in your left hand so that the White/Green core is at the top.

(If you are left handed, reverse this). Slide the cores into the rear of the Modular Plug. If the cores are all lying flat and straight, you should find that they are guided smoothly into their separate channels. Push the cores in firmly so that they butt fully against the end of the plug.

6. With the cable fully butted into the plug, insert the plug into the termination tool and crimp to complete the termination. You can then slide any strain relief components along the cable and onto the back of the plug.

Testing the Twisted Pair Cabling

In order to test the twisted pair cabling system, we need to check electrical continuity between the pins on the Modular Plugs at either end of the link between the hub and the PC. As these plugs are likely to be at some distance from each other, testing across the length of the link will be difficult with a normal hand held Multimeter. The solution to this problem is to make a simple 'loop back' plug.

This plug will be fitted into the Outlet Module and will connect the appropriate pairs of connection links together at the Outlet Module. This link completes the circuit at the Outlet Module, allowing us to test for continuity across the appropriate contacts at the hub-end Modular Plug.

Make up the 'loop back' plugs as follows:

1. Terminate a length of UTP cable with a Modular Plug as before and then cut the cable at about 5cm from the back of the plug. You will find it easier to do it this way, rather than to try and terminate a short length.

2. Remove about 3 cm of the cable sleeving from the end of the cable, being careful as before not to damage the core insulation underneath. Separate the twisted pairs.

3. Then, one at a time untwist each pair, strip the insulation from the core to expose the copper and then twist the bare copper

cores firmly back together so that Green/White connects to White/Green and so on. Cover each exposed contact with some tape to prevent shorting.

With this loop back plug, you can then test each link one at a time by inserting the loop back plug into the Outlet Module and testing for continuity using the Multimeter across the contacts at the hub-end Modular Plug that corresponds to the outlet.

Using the standard numbering system where, with the cable down and the metal contacts on the Modular Plug facing you, the left end pin is No. 1 and the right end pin is No. 8 test for continuity across the following contacts:

- i&2 – Green pair
- 3&6 – Orange pair
- 4&5 – Blue pair
- 7&8 – Brown pair

Ethernet Hubs

Ethernet hubs are available in a wide variety of formats. The types suitable for twisted pair Ethernet operation and known as 10BaseT or 100BaseT hubs, depending on the Ethernet speed. The 'I0 or 'I00' refers to the operating frequency (10Mhz or 100Mhz); the 'Base' refers to baseband which is the type of signalling used and the 'T' refers to twisted pair.

10BaseT hubs are available as either rack mounted (which are designed to fit standard networking equipment racks) or desktop (which are designed to sit freely on a desktop or shelf). Rack mounted hubs are mainly used in large scale networks, whereas desktop hubs are more suitable for the small office environment.

Desktop hubs contain either four or (more usually) eight Ethernet ports.

The simplest eight port hubs are the perfectly adequate for our needs.

Other features that you may find are hubs that are SNMP compatible or that integrate other types of Ethernet ports for connection to other types of Ethernet media (e.g., Fibre optics). SNMP stands for Simple Network Management Protocol an advanced system that allows for a standardised form of network management.

Stackable Hubs

One feature that is available for Ethernet hubs and may be useful is the ability to stack hubs together. This allows for the number of ports available to the network to be increased by connecting further hubs to the existing hub in a 'stacking' arrangement. This facility therefore allows for each expansion of the initial network configuration as the need arises.

3

Designing Your Network

Introduction

Given the recent surge in networking, it might be possible to believe that you could build a network simply by purchasing the parts and following the instructions that explain how to insert tab A into slot B and so forth. It is possible to purchase the parts and assemble them into a network.

However, if you are working with a business or organizational network, and you want to get started on the right foot, it is necessary to approach the various sets of instructions you will receive, with products, in books, advice from friends, etc.

Identifying the Uses of Your Network

Every network is different. Just as every human being is different. Once created a network grows its own way. No matter what your organization does, its network has to accomplish only one task to be considered successful. It has to ensure that what your organization does, it can do better, faster, more efficiently, and more reliably with the assistance of a network.

If the network does not work do that, it will be a failure, regardless of the quantity of premium technology and quality of service. Keep this is mind as you progress, it is the single most important fact here. The network is not about technology, no matter how much a techo-fanatic may want it to be.

Networks are about getting things done, primarily by people who could not care less whether they do their work on a network or not.

Deciding What Happens at Which Computer

The next step in the network-design process seems obvious. This is knowing which applications and tasks have to preformed at each of the computers on your network. There can be various options under it. Some of them are:

Many-User Computer

Computers used by many users can be built minimally or with all the bells and whistles As with any other system, the amount of power and features depends on the application.

Single-User Computers

It generally occurs in offices. Whether an office is physical or virtual, an increasing number of office workers use computers on a day-to-day basis. This shift in computer has created a new class of office workers called knowledge workers because their currency is dealing with information and formatting, managing, and analyzing data.

Given the increasing focus on high-tech jobs and high-tech workforces, it is easy to lose sight of the fact that knowledge workers are not a homogeneous mass.

Depending on the nature of their jobs, they tend to require higher-end computers to begin with, but they also have widely varying connectivity requirements. For example, some workers may be able to leave their work behind at the end of the day and require no remote access; other users may require two or more computers to be able to do their jobs.

Naturally, this is a rightsizing issue, if you have to provide more than one computer for some users, it is going to affect your capacity planning to a great degree.

Determining the Degree of Centralization

There are times to centralize administration and security, and there are times not to. There are times when it is worthwhile to go the whole nine yards toward establishing a central administrative authority, and times when the return from doing so is not worth the effort or expense. When you are designing a network, you must determine whether or not you want the ability to administer your network from a central point.

Clearly, you would not necessarily want to administer every system if your network consists of only a few computers (less than 10 or so) in the same location. The cost of network management software, that can handle configuration management and software distribution, among other tasks, is altogether too high to justify on a small, local network. On the other hand, even for a small network, you may want to find some way of centralizing some functions such as file services, security, and backup.

Client/server networks, by contrast, are secure. Their files are usually stored in a central location and backed up on a regular basis. User tends to be controllable. As a result, there are myriad upsides of even basic centralization.

1. Easier access to files
2. Stronger security
3. Easier backup
4. Easier configuration management and standardization of workstations.

Easier access to files

Files stored across multiple workstations can present a problem for network users. If the user has to put together a contract, he or she might have to find a contract file stored on server's machine. To centralize access to files, you have to build a file server, or a server dedicated to sharing its disk space with a collection of users for file storage. Typically, a file server requires a powerful processor, a lot of memory, and as much disk space as you can afford.

Stronger Security

File servers usually have some security built in so that they can ensure that access to files is limited to those users who should have access to them.

Typically, file server security for PC-based operating systems follow some fairly simple rules:

1. Security inheritance works similarly to financial inheritance; what a parent has can by a child unless it is blocked by third parties. In security a user gets access to a particular directory. Whatever access a user has to this directory is inherited by any and all subdirectories of this directory. Inheritance is a useful tool to ensure that a user has as much access as he or she requires to a given part of the server's disk.
2. In general, uses are limited to 3 levels of access to a given file or directory on a file server:

   No Access, which often means that users cannot even see the file or directory.

   Read-only Access, which means that users can view the contents of a file or directory but cannot modify it.

   Read-write Access, which means that a user has the access rights to view and modify files and directories.

Easier Backup

If all the network user's files are stored on a centralized server, they can be backed up simply by duplicating the server's hard drive to tape. Assuming that your network has 50 user workstations. If all the users store their files on their workstations, you will have to back up all or part of their hard drives to ensure that no data is lost if a system crashes.

Further suppose that each user has 25 megabytes of files on their workstation's hard drives. Backing up this quantity of files across the network for this many users could take 10 or 12 hours and be a nightmare to manage.

On the other hand backing up to a server's drive with an attached tape drive can take as little as an hour or so. Clearly, backing up files from a single server to a tape drive takes less time is more controllable.

Easier Configuration Management

It is an art of using a central console to ensure that user workstations have the correct hardware and software installed, and that the software and hardware are set up according to consensus and preset standards. Its software is however, little complex. It is usually composed of a highly complex database with a proprietary front end that allows a network administrator to view and modify the configurations workstations.

Most management software requires that each system have an agent installed on the workstation, often, agents can be installed automatically as a user logs on the network.

Drawing the Network

By this time you have gained knowledge about:

- ☐ The purpose of the network
- ☐ The specifies of the network's use
- ☐ The quantity of both users and computers
- ☐ Whether or not the network will be centralised or decentralised
- ☐ The network topology you plant to use

Drawing the Logical Diagram

The first drawing you make is the logical diagram. It details the applications that have to run on workstations have to be able to access.

1. Start by drawing a workstation for each type of user (for example, one warehouse floor computer, one analyst's computer, one accounting computer, one secretary's computer and so on). Just make a circle for each computer; draw them in a line across the top of the whiteboard or page.
2. Below each computer, list the applications it has to run. This could include word processing, spreadsheets, emails, scheduling and more for a user's desktop computer, or a single application for a dedicated machine, such as a factory or warehouse inventory computer or an in-office computer dedicated to routing email.
3. Make a list of the resources each workstation computer will share. In general, peer networking has a lot of these shared resources (such as printers, scanners, shared modems and so on); client/server networks will have fewer shared resources. No matter whether you've elected to use client/server or peer, add these resources into your diagram.
4. If the system will participate in a network-wide security scheme, note which group of users has login access to the various pieces of the system. For example, business desktop users can log into the file server, warehouse supervisors can log into the transaction server and administrators can log in to anything anywhere. This step helps ensure that you provide the correct levels of security.
5. Add the workstation operating system to the bottom of the list. The Operating System is usually something like MS-DOS, Windows, or Macintosh. Although Unix can be used as a client, outside of academic computing centers and high-end engineering workstations, it is not common as a workstation Operating System, ensure that you have more than one computer drawn–each workstation Operating System should be shown on a separate machine.

6. Add the quantity of each type of workstation to the bottom of the list.

   Now your workstations are quantified. If you are going to build a client/server network and will require one or more servers, add the servers in at the bottom of the diagram and list the applications and resources each server provides to the network. If you are building a WAN and have to incorporate routers and so forth to hook the LANs together, draw the routers in at the side.

   Now comes the fun part. Draw lines from each workstation type to each system to which that workstation type requires access. In other words, if an accounting PC requires file storage resources on a file server, select a colored marker, draw a line between the two systems and write the name of the resource the workstation client will use.

   If a workstation has a shared printer, ensure that other systems that have to use it are connected to it using lines of a different color than the first. If a router provides connectivity between the network and the workstations, but must first route data through a server, draw that full path as well in yet another color.

Drawing the Physical Network Diagram

Drawing the physical network really isn't as hard as it sounds. If you already know which clients have to be connected to specific resources and which topology you'll be using, you're halfway there.

1. Start by drawing the physical center of your network.

   If you're using a star configuration (such as Ethernet, Token Ring or FDDI), the center of your network is the concentrator: a hub, MAU or switch of some sort. If your network needs only one hub, draw a box and label it as the hub.

2. Draw as many boxes as you will have shared media hubs. (Keep in mind that hubs are measured by the number of ports they have; an 8-port hub supports eight workstations, 16 ports support

16 workstations, and so forth). For performance reasons, it's a good idea to divide the network into single hubs with no more than 16 ports per segment. Connect lines between the switch and the segments; each of these lines represents a crossover cable, or a specially made cable that can be used to connect concentrators together.

3. Draw the servers and mark them as connected directly to the switch. A server connected directly to a switch offers compelling advantages in terms of performance at the workstation because the server has a direct connection to the port to which the workstation is connected.

   This holds true even if a workstation is connected through a hub connected to a switch port; the collision domain of individual hubs are usually fairly small, so there isn't much competition for bandwidth.

4. Refer to the drawing of the logical network and do some analysis. Look at which workstations require access to which servers and try to group them together.

5. Once you analyze the relative bandwidth requirements of your users, you're ready to start figuring out which class of user has to connect to which device.

Take the time to think about this. If users don't have sufficient bandwidth initially, they will have network problems and consequently lose faith in the network. It's important to roll out systems that work for the users, otherwise the network has no credibility.

Writing Specification & Getting Other's Input

Once you've gotten this far, you have enough data to write a document that includes the following:

- ☐ The organisational purpose of the network
- ☐ The specifics of the network's use

- ☐ The quantity of both users and computers
- ☐ Whether or not the network will be centralized or decentralized
- ☐ The network topology you plan to use

You also have a pair of diagrams that portray the logical and physical connections required by network. Pat yourself on the back – you deserve it. You've created the basis for an initial specification document, which enumerates all the preceding points and includes the diagrams.

Writing the Specification Document

Now is the time to actually write your specification for the network. The specification document should take into account all the points in the preceding section and list, quite specifically, the various users of the network. Specifications do not have to be long, but they must be complete and clear; as English teachers are prone to say, "It should be as long as it needs to be – but no longer."

SPECIFYING HARDWARE

Until this point, the network-planning process has dealt entirely with use and software application issues. At this point, you should know what the network needs to do, but you haven't begun looking at hardware products …at least, not specifically.

Selecting Hardware

Networking hardware typically comes in two configurations: the latest and greatest hub/switch/chasis that costs. If the network you are building is small and not slated to expand, the cheaper is acceptable; it will provide basic connectivity and adequate performance.

If your network is expanding, try to get as much capacity as possible because doing so buys you breathing space. Because networking technology changes so rapidly, purchasing excess capacity is often the only way to get a full, useful life span out of equipment.

It's not a terribly platable decision to make, but unfortunately it's the dirty little secret of networking hardware capacity planning.

The following list provides a baseline for the physical part of your network. This list doesn't provide specific recommendations because hardware changes so rapidly. But it does tell you the features you're like to find useful.

Network Interface Cards

For each computer, you need at least one network card. NICs can cost as little as Rs.2000 or as much as Rs.15000. Make certain that your network cards are the correct topology; even through Token-Ring cards have the same network-cable connector as Ethernet 10BASE-T cards, Ethernet cards won't work on Token-Ring networks and vice versa.

Concentrators (MAUs, hubs and switches)

Once you know how many computers will be on your network, you know how many ports you need. Once you know how many ports you require, it's a matter of determining whether they will be switched or shared media, as detailed (in the abstract) in the specification you've already created.

Wiring

If you're using a star-configuration network, you'll have to run cables from the wiring closet in which the hubs are stored to each workstation's location. Ensure that you use at least Category 5 or better twisted-pair wire; even at twice the price of the lower cable certifications such as Category 3, it's cheap because it has a longer useful life span.

If you're using a bus-configuration network, you'll have to run coaxial cable serially between workstations. If you decide to install the cable yourself, remember to handle it gently, regardless of whether it's coax or twisted pair. Treating the wire gently (that is, not crimping or breaking it) helps ensure that you'll get a better connection. A better solution, if your organisation has the finances, is to hire someone who runs cable for a living. Electricians are often smaller cable installers because they run so many cables through walls and other inaccessible locations.

Workstation computers

Once you have specified your network cards, hubs and cables, you're ready to spec out your computers. Refer to the specification you wrote to determine which users need powerful workstations and which ones can use lower-end systems and specify them. Because hardware changes so rapidly, it's pointless to create a fixed specification here, but as of 2001, the fastest chips are reaching 1 gigahertz speeds, so workstations in the 600 to 850 Mhz range are fine for now.

Don't consider this recommendation to be a standard; see what the market is offering. What constitutes a powerful PC changes incredibly fast, so do research to find out what's currently available in the market and that too at a reasonable price.

Server computers

By the same token, overbuild your servers. Get as much power a machine as you can afford and add as much memory as possible. No matter what your application, the power and memory you provide will be used in six months or less and will be tight in a year or so. Figure out your server's disk-space requirements (a good minimum is 100 Mb per user; more is always better) and then double it if possible. Don't worry; the disk space will be used – probably sooner than you expect.

Management features

When you purchase your hardware, ensure that it can support the SNMP or RMON network-management standard. Even if you don't use the management features immediately, as your network grows, SNMP and RMON capability can extend the useful life of a piece of equipment by ensuring that it can be managed as part of a greater network.

Other features

Likewise, try to find working hardware that can support advanced features like VLANs. Having the capability is crucial because it ensures that you have options. The more options your hardware has, the more it prevents your networking hardware from becoming quickly obsolete.

Building the Network

Once you've settled on the hardware; you're ready to begin building the network.

4

CONFIGURING WINDOWS FOR NETWORKING

NTRODUCTION

ince we are talking about PCs as our computers used for etworking and Windows as the operating system, we must onfigure Windows to use it for networking for our PC attached to ach other through networking.

ollowing are the various steps that you will take to configure your Vindows operating system for networking.

NSTALLING MICROSOFT NETWORK

o do this proceed as following:

Click at Start menu. Click at Settings, Control Panel and Networks.

A dialog box, as shown on the next page, is given to you.

A list of installed components of networking are shown here.

Click at the entry called Client for Microsoft Networks.

If not present you can it by using the button called ADD.

From the dialog box which appears, double click at client.

From the list of manufacturers, select Microsoft.

From the list of Network Clients, select Client for Microsoft Networks.

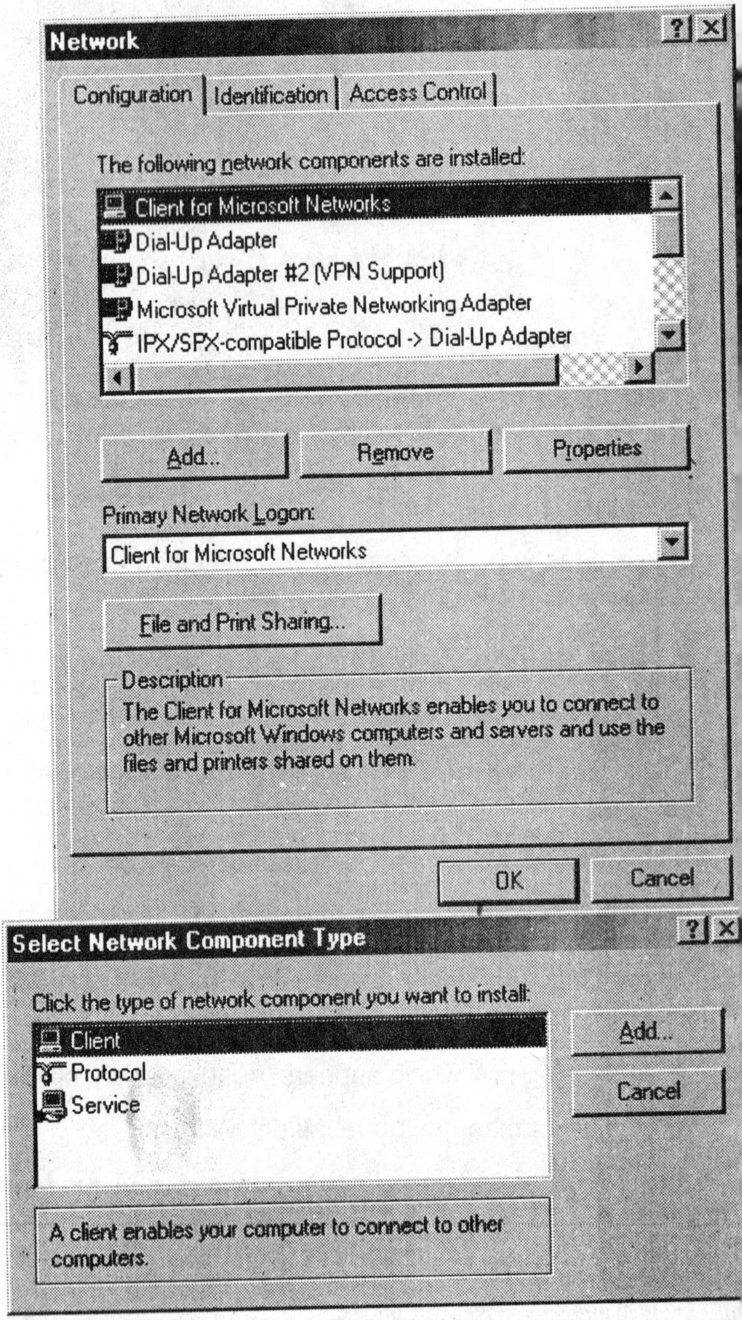
Network
Configuration
Identification
Access Control
The following network components are installed:
Client for Microsoft Networks
Dial-Up Adapter
Dial-Up Adapter #2 (VPN Support)
Microsoft Virtual Private Networking Adapter
IPX/SPX-compatible Protocol -> Dial-Up Adapter
Add...
Remove
Properties
Primary Network Logon:
Client for Microsoft Networks
File and Print Sharing...
Description
The Client for Microsoft Networks enables you to connect to other Microsoft Windows computers and servers and use the files and printers shared on them.
OK
Cancel
Select Network Component Type
Click the type of network component you want to install:
Client
Protocol
Service
Add...
Cancel
A client enables your computer to connect to other computers.

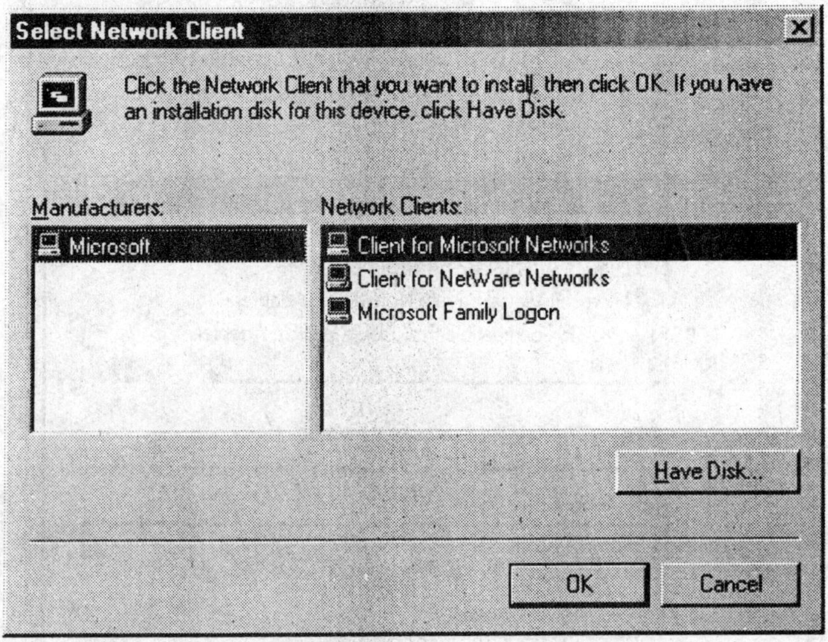

9. Click Ok to have the same.
10. Now your list will have Client for Microsoft Networks.

Installing Protocols

The protocol that is required for immediate communication between PCs on the network is the NetBEUI protocol. Windows also supports other protocols for this purpose, but in preference we will use the NetBEUI protocol as this is specifically designed for Windows network communications.

To install the NetBEUI driver, proceed as follows:

1. Open the Network dialog box using Start menu and Settings and Control Panel.
2. This is shown on the next page.
3. Click at Add.

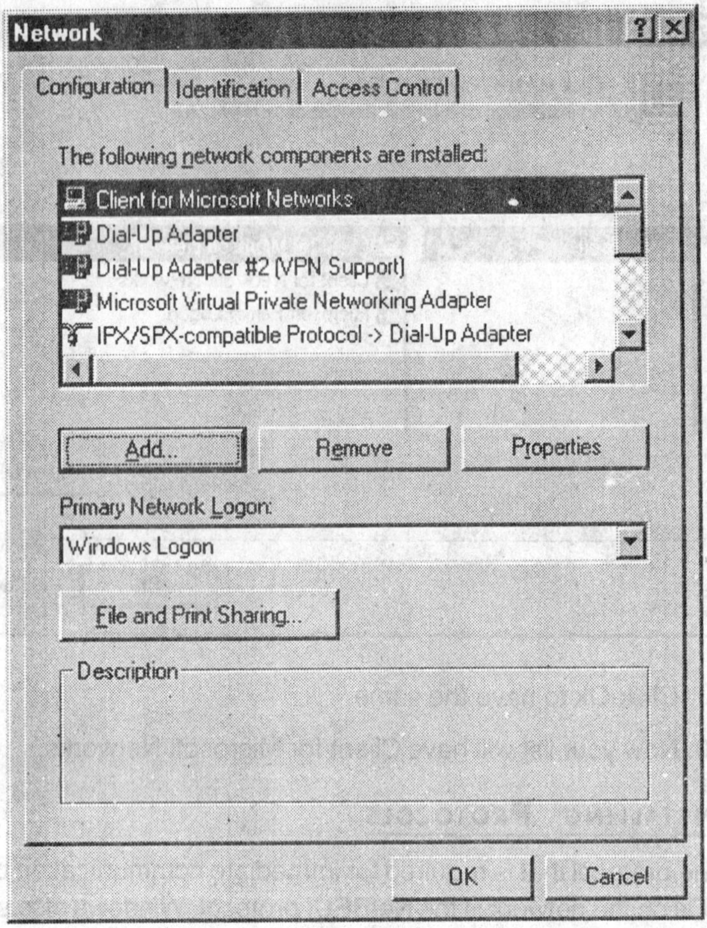

4. Select and double click Protocol.
5. Select Microsoft from the list of manufacturers.
6. Select NetBEUI from the list of Network Protocols.
7. Click Ok.

If the TCP/IP is not installed, install it now by repeating the above steps. On installing the protocol driver, you will be prompted to restart Windows or you can proceed further.

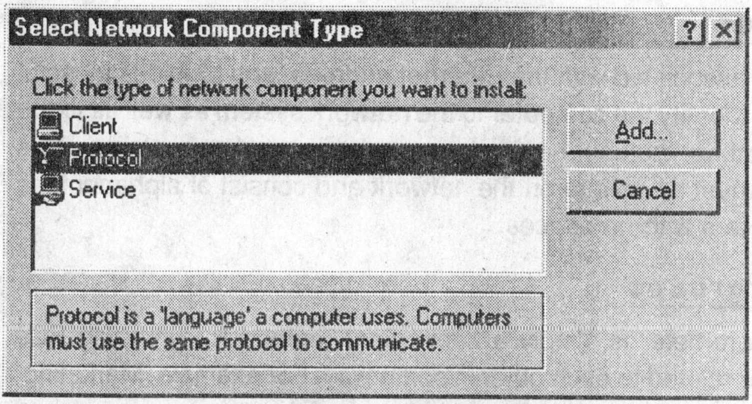

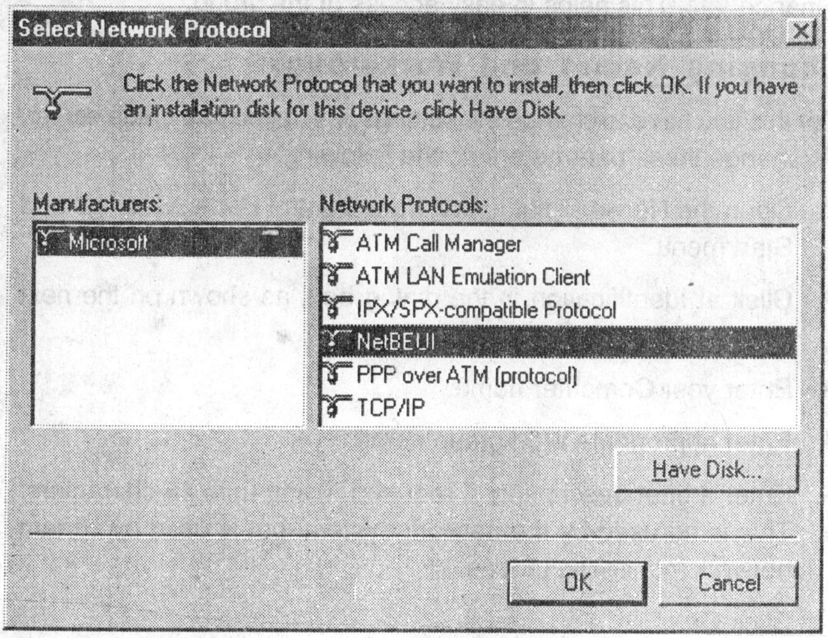

Understanding Names and Workgroups

After the initial installation these names are then available to various advanced Windows utilities for defining and customizing things like desktop settings and security policies.

Let us see how each one of them can be changed.

Names

This is associated with the Ethernet address, and provides a useful way to identify the computer to the network system as well as to the user without the user having to use complex coding systems. This name must be unique on the network and consist of alphanumeric characters with no spaces.

Workgroups

This parameter is simply a convenient method for grouping PCs that are related to each other in some way. For example, Marketing, Finance, etc. This helps in easy access of the group.

Changing Names and Workgroups

For this you have to change the settings which you had made earlier. To change these parameters do the following:

1. Open the Network dialog box from Control Panel, Settings and Start menu.
2. Click at Identification in the dialog box, as shown on the next page.
3. Enter your Computer name.
4. Enter appropriate Workgroup name.
5. Enter a brief description, if required, using upto 48 characters. This is no used by the network system, but is used by certain network monitoring utilities.
6. Click Ok.

Installing File and Printer Sharing

So far we have setup to share the computers. Now we will set up to share the files and printers. This will allow other users on the network to access file on your PC hard disk and printers attached to your PC subject to other security allowances.

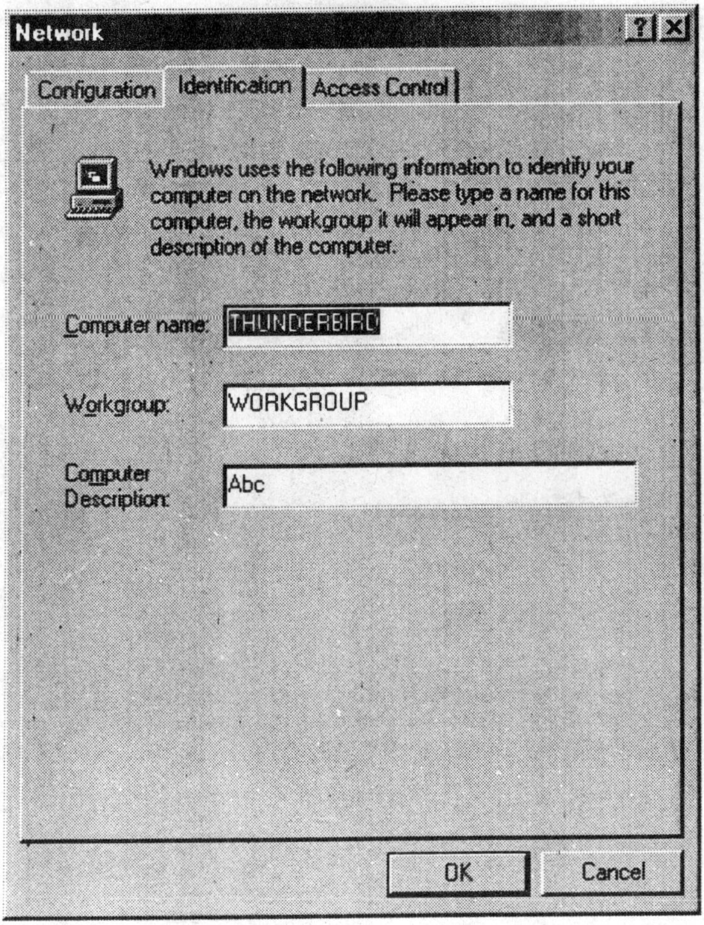

To do this follow the following steps.

1. Open the network dialog box, as done in earlier cases.
2. This time click at File and printer sharing for Microsoft Networks.
3. If not present, click at Add.
4. From the list of Network clients, select File and printer sharing for Microsoft Networks.
5. Click Ok.

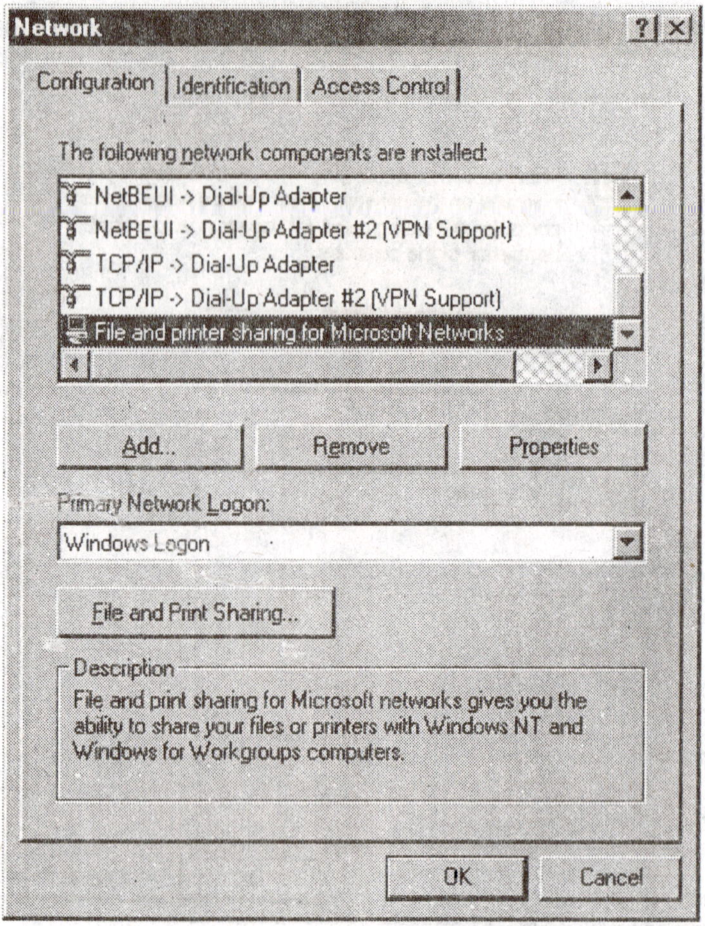

6. Now back in Network dialog box, click at File and Printer Sharing in the Network window.
7. This would lead to another dialog box, as shown on the next page.
8. Here ensure that both 'I want to give others access to my files' and 'I want to be able to allow others to print to my printer(s)' are checked.
9. Click on Ok and then click on Ok in the Network dialog box. This

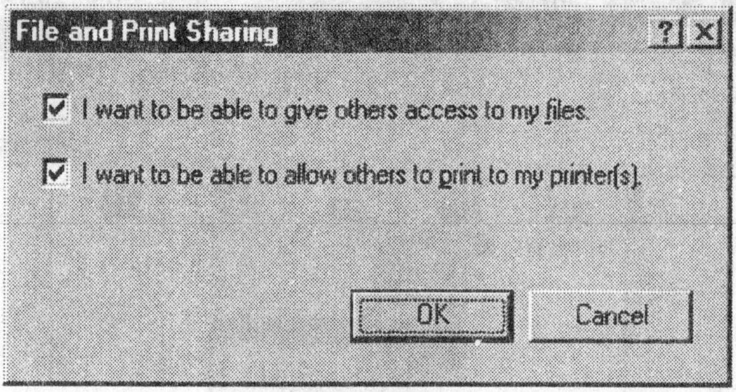

being the final setting, when prompted to restart Windows, answer Yes.

SHARING LEVEL SECURITY

A source of a PC can be shared or not. A resource can be any disk drive, directory, file, or peripheral device such as a printer or modem that is attached via a PC interface to the network. Once a resource is defined as shared, it can then be further defined as changeable or not. The resource can also be protected from unauthorised access if required by defining a password for that resource.

If you make an entire disk drive available as shared then all the directories and files in that disk drive automatically become available. If however, you only require certain directories on a disk drive be available across the network, then the entire disk must be defined as unshared but with each individual directory that is intented to be accessible being defined as shared separately.

To enable sharing of a particular disk based resouce, do the following:

1. From the Windows desktop, double click at My Computer.
2. Select the resource you wish to enable for sharing for directories and files, double click again.
3. Right click on the resource and then click at Sharing.
4. This will give rise to a dialog box.

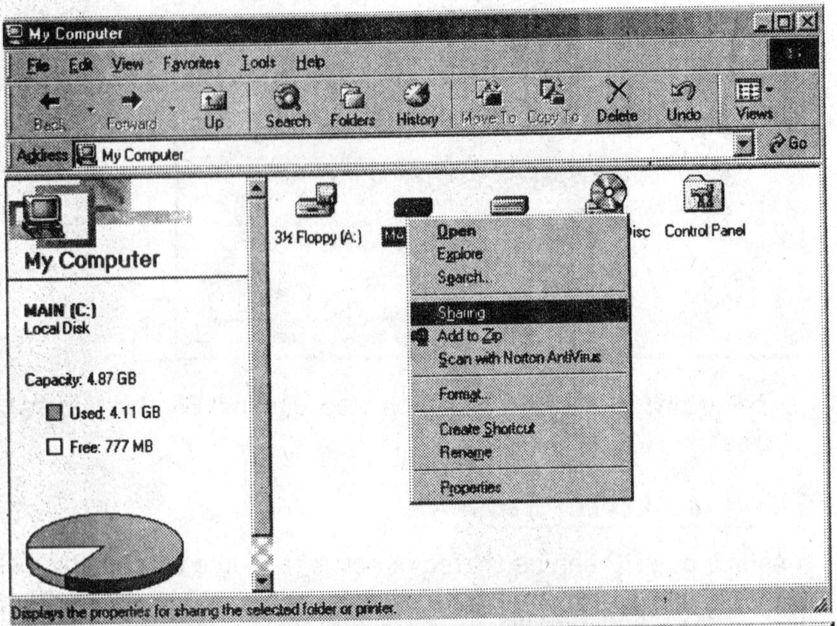
My Computer
File Edit View Favorites Tools Help
Back Forward Up Search Folders History Move To Copy To Delete Undo Views
Address My Computer
Go
My Computer
MAIN (C:)
Local Disk
Capacity: 4.87 GB
Used: 4.11 GB
Free: 777 MB
3½ Floppy (A:)
Control Panel
Open
Explore
Search...
Sharing
Add to Zip
Scan with Norton AntiVirus
Format...
Create Shortcut
Rename
Properties
Displays the properties for sharing the selected folder or printer.

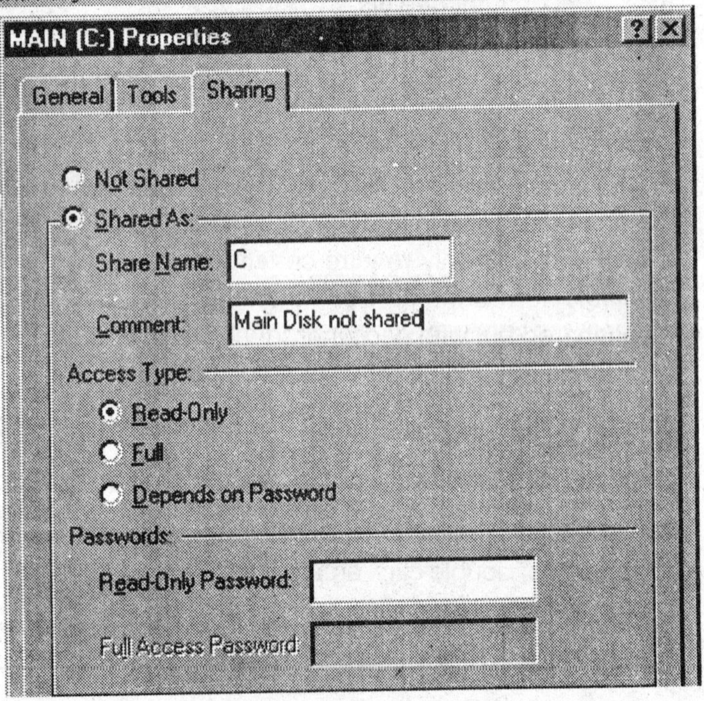
MAIN (C:) Properties
General
Tools
Sharing
Not Shared
Shared As:
Share Name:
C
Comment:
Main Disk not shared
Access Type:
Read-Only
Full
Depends on Password
Passwords:
Read-Only Password:
Full Access Password:

5. Enter an alternative name for the shared resource if required. This will be the main reference name. You may add a comment if you wish.

6. For limited access with no password, select Read only. If you wish to restrict Read only access you can enter a Read only password in the box provided. Click Ok. If you specify a password for Read only access, you will then be prompted to confirm this.

7. If full access is required, select Full. Once again, if you require a password restriction to full access you can specify this in the

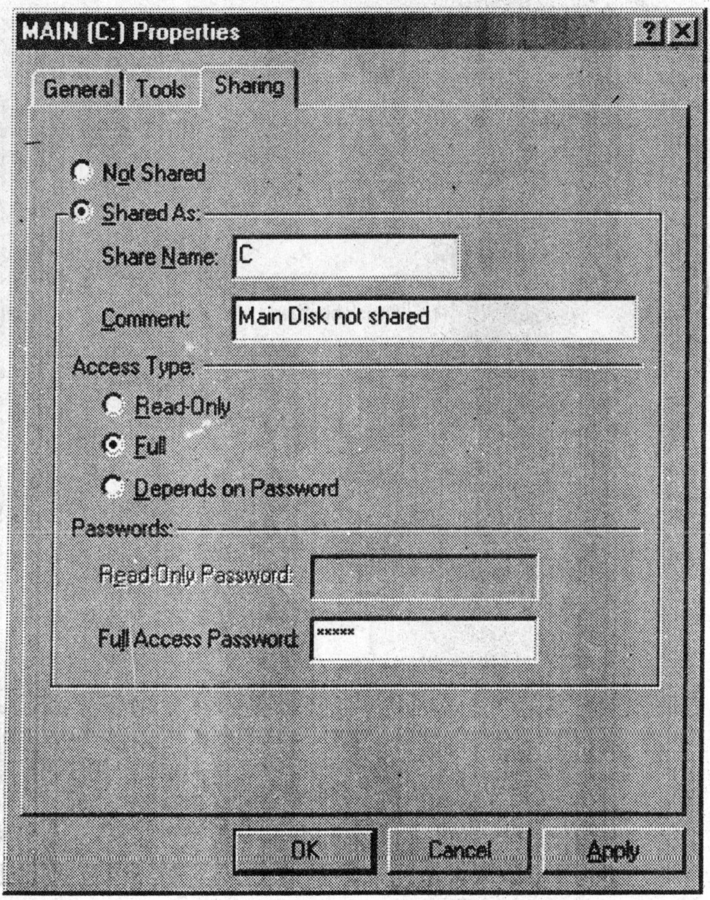

box provided. Click Ok. If you specified a password, you will be prompted to confirm this.

8. You also have the option to control which type of access is granted depending on different passwords. If you select Depends on Password you can then enter two different passwords. When access to this resource is subsequently requested, the type of access granted will depend on which of the two passwords was entered. This can be useful, for example if the Read only password is given to users of a particular resource, whilst the Full access password is given to mangers of that resource. Once

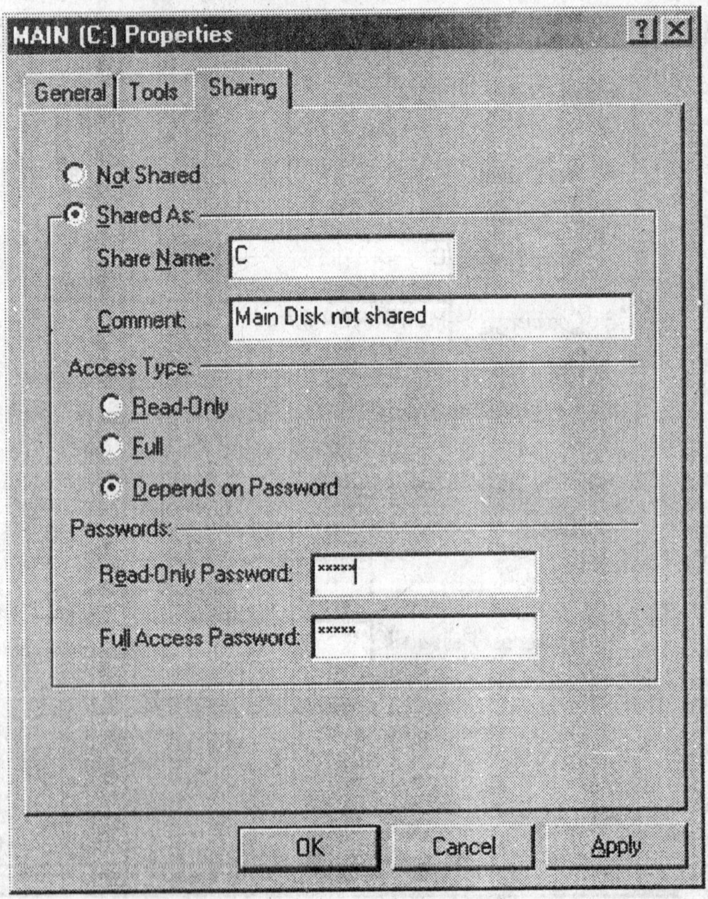

again, on clicking Ok you will be prompted to confirm both password.

PRINTER SHARING

Now we understand how a printer can be shared across the networks. Once a printer is shared on the networking, it is called the Network printer. This network printer must be added to the list of available printers on the any remote PCs.

For this follow the following steps:

1. Click at Printers in the Control Panel to get the printers dialog box.

2. Right click on the printer that your wish to share. If no printers are available, you will need to define one using the Add Printer wizard.

3. Click on Sharing.

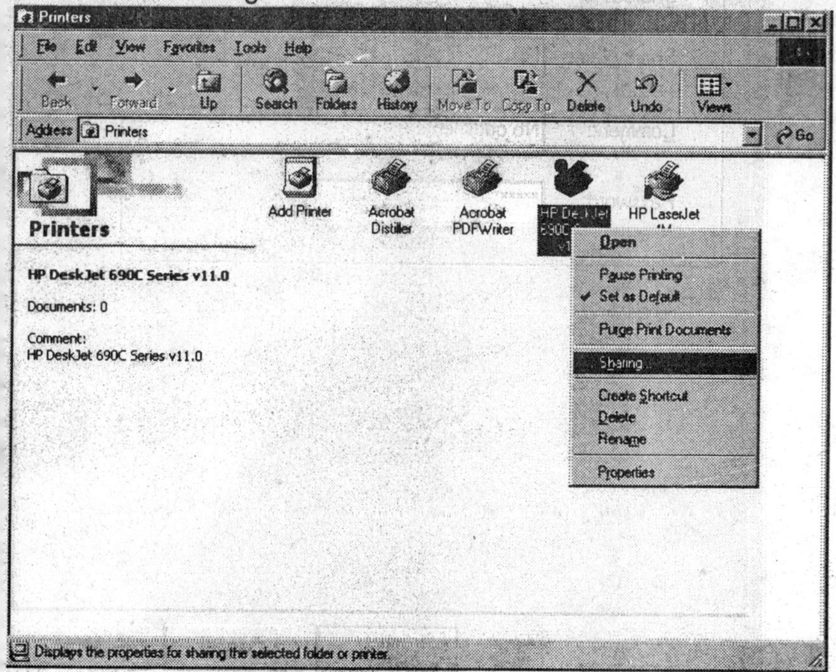

4. Click on Shared As. You can then enter a name for your network printer.
5. If required, you can also enter a password for access to the printer across the network.
6. Click on Ok. If you have entered a password, you will now be prompted to confirm it.

Having defined a printer as shared on the PC to which it is attached, we must then add this printer to the list of available printer to the list

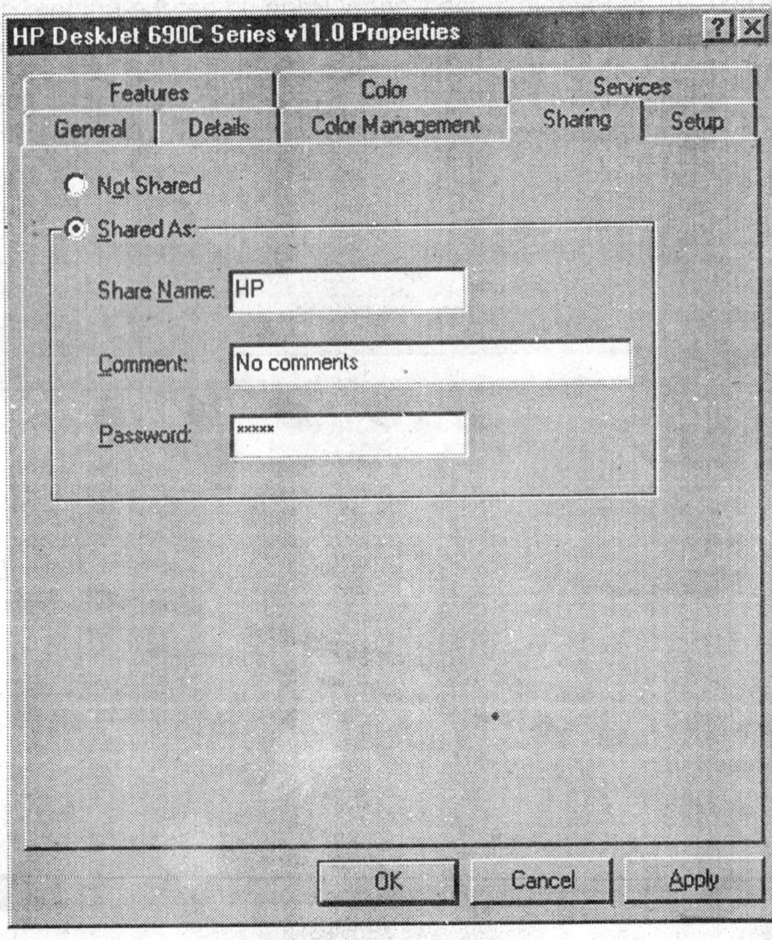

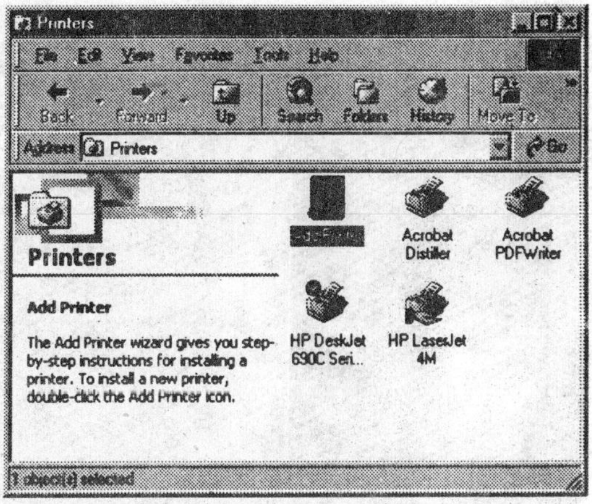

of available printers on each PC that wishes to gain access to the shared network printer.

1. Get the printers dialog box from the control panel.
2. Double click at Add printer.
3. A printer wizard will start, which will ask you various questions before installing the printer.
4. These steps are shown in the form of dialog boxes on the next few pages.
5. These are self defining and do not need any other explanations.

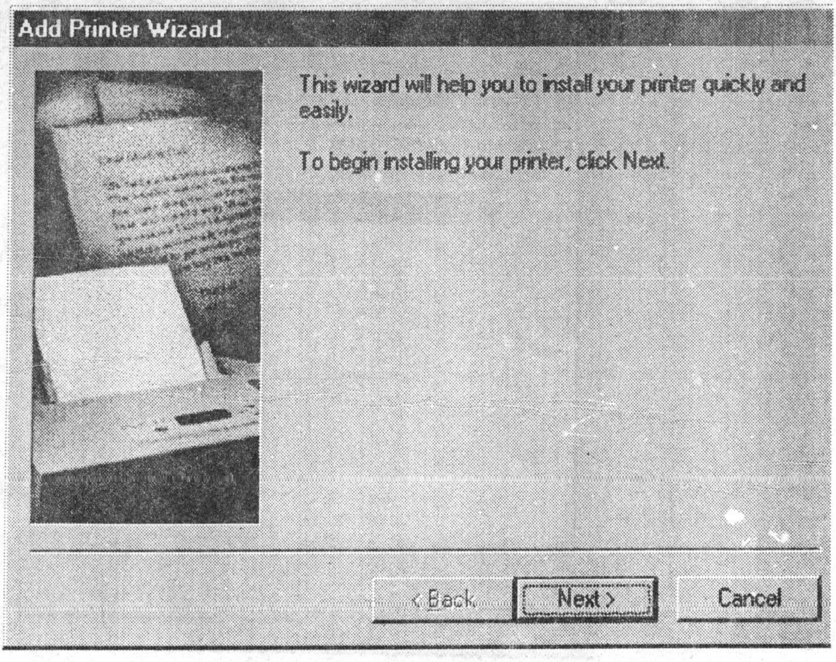

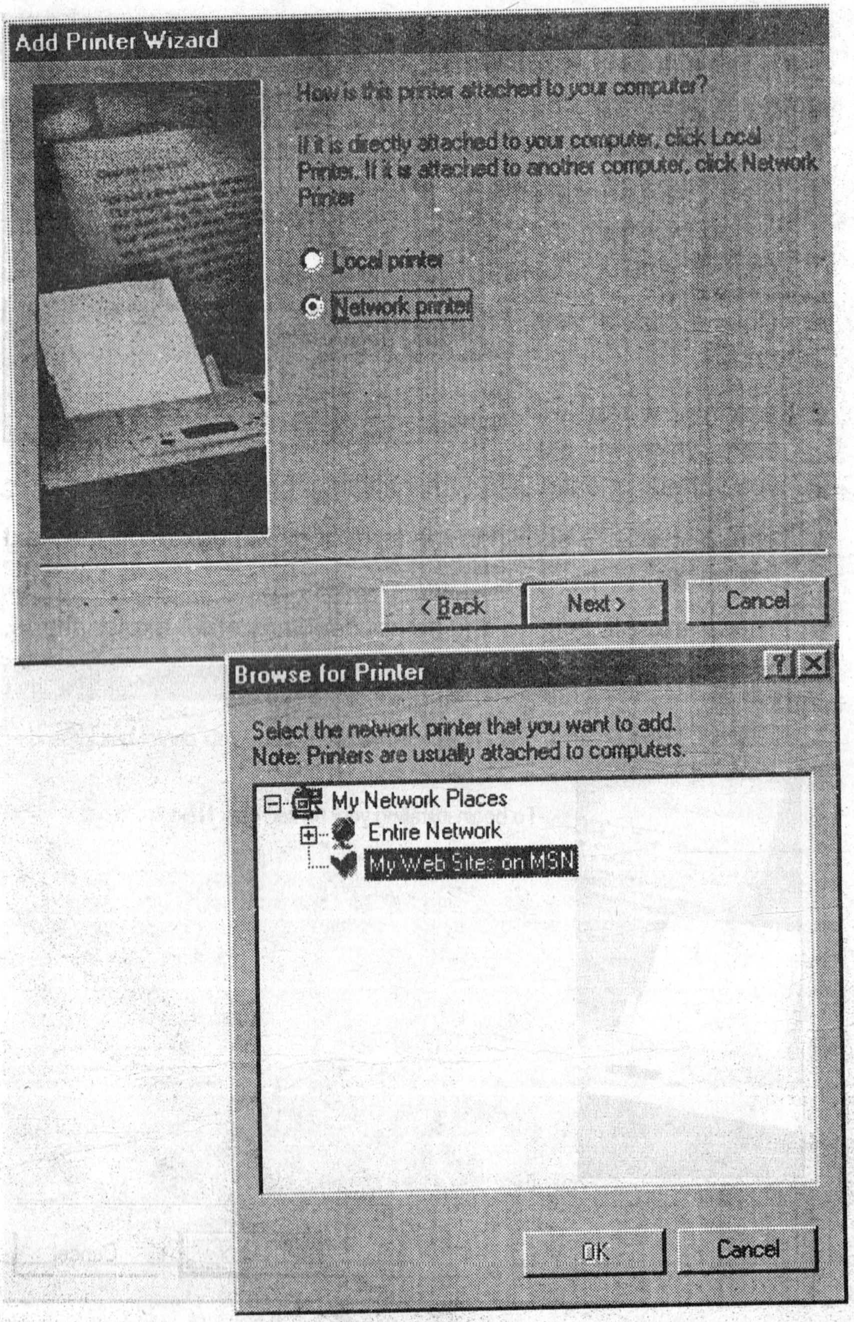
Add Printer Wizard
How is this printer attached to your computer?
If it is directly attached to your computer, click Local Printer. If it is attached to another computer, click Network Printer
Local printer
Network printer
< Back
Next >
Cancel
Browse for Printer
Select the network printer that you want to add.
Note: Printers are usually attached to computers.
My Network Places
Entire Network
My Web Sites on MSN
OK
Cancel

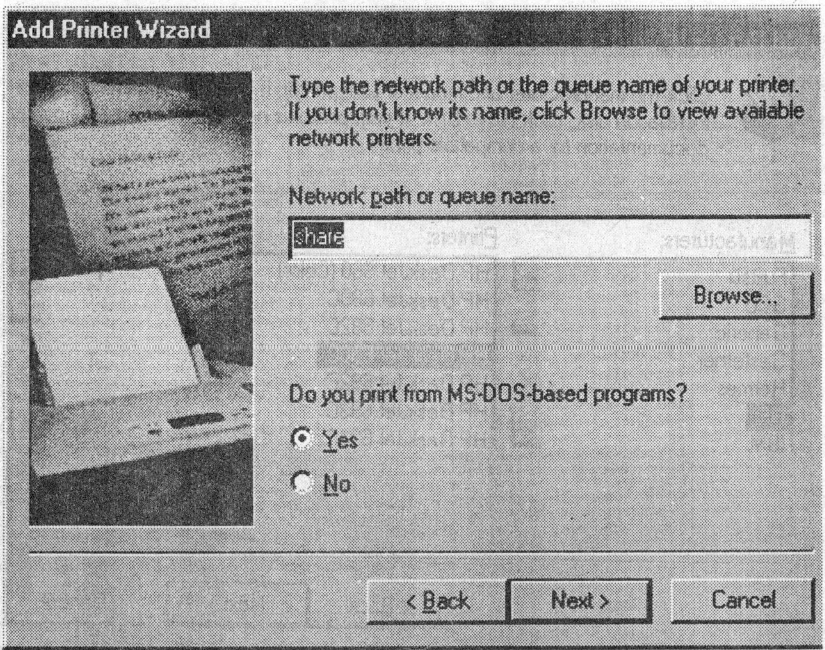
Add Printer Wizard
Type the network path or the queue name of your printer. If you don't know its name, click Browse to view available network printers.
Network path or queue name:
share
Browse...
Do you print from MS-DOS-based programs?
Yes
No
< Back
Next >
Cancel

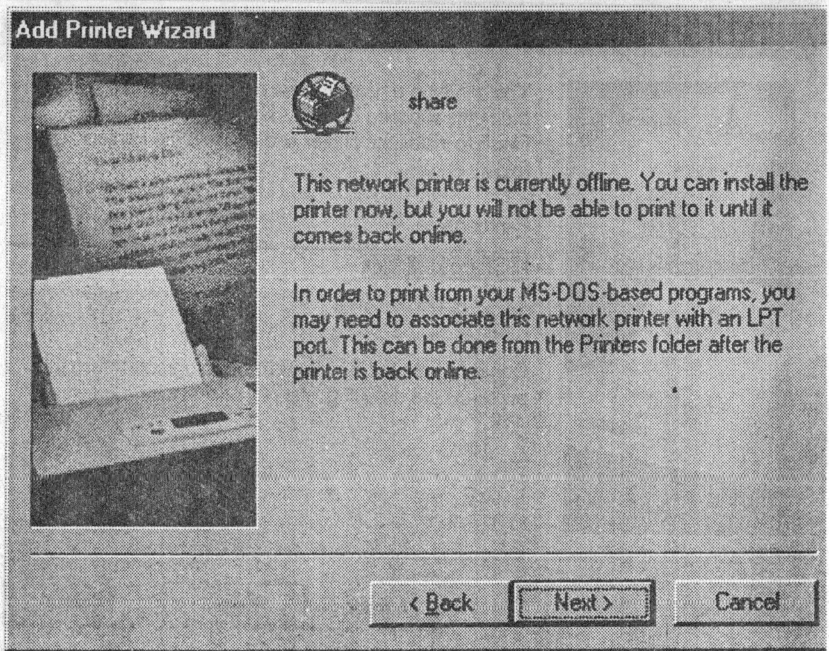
Add Printer Wizard
share
This network printer is currently offline. You can install the printer now, but you will not be able to print to it until it comes back online.
In order to print from your MS-DOS-based programs, you may need to associate this network printer with an LPT port. This can be done from the Printers folder after the printer is back online.
< Back
Next >
Cancel

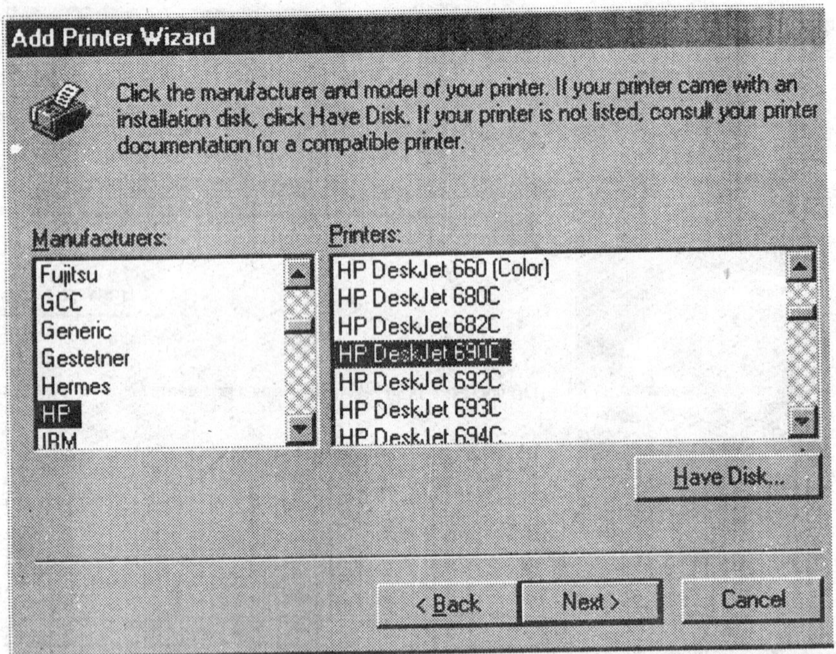
Add Printer Wizard
Click the manufacturer and model of your printer. If your printer came with an installation disk, click Have Disk. If your printer is not listed, consult your printer documentation for a compatible printer.
Manufacturers:
Fujitsu
GCC
Generic
Gestetner
Hermes
HP
IBM
Printers:
HP DeskJet 660 (Color)
HP DeskJet 680C
HP DeskJet 682C
HP DeskJet 690C
HP DeskJet 692C
HP DeskJet 693C
HP DeskJet 694C
Have Disk...
< Back
Next >
Cancel

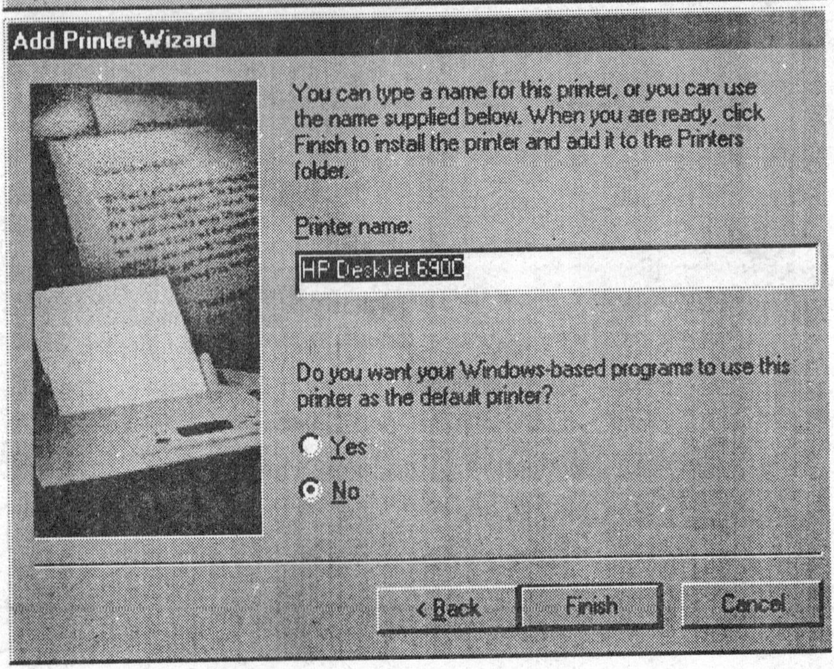
Add Printer Wizard
You can type a name for this printer, or you can use the name supplied below. When you are ready, click Finish to install the printer and add it to the Printers folder.
Printer name:
HP DeskJet 690C
Do you want your Windows-based programs to use this printer as the default printer?
Yes
No
< Back
Finish
Cancel

5

Setting up Hardware for Internet

Introduction

Now let us understand the process of setting up the hardware to connecting to the Internet. We will in this chapter go through the various items required in the form of hardware and setting up of them.

Understanding Internet Access

Since we are reading in this book about networking, so we would try to concentrate on accessing the Internet through multi-user networking environment.

Connecting to the Internet is simply a process of allowing your computer to communicate with another specialised computer that is dedicated to providing this service and is permanently connected to the Internet. This specialised remote computer is normally provided by an Internet Service Provider or ISP, type of vendors who provide you with the Internet connection, for example, VSNL, etc.

As the overwhelming majority of Internet communications is via the TCP/IP (Transmission Control Protocol/Internet Protocol) protocol, you must also be using this protocol in order to establish a communication channel with the Internet via an ISP.

There are 3 main types of hardware that are commonly used to connect to the Internet. The choice of which type best suits your needs will depend primarily on how fast you want your connection to operate at and whether or not you require access for a single user or for a group of users on a network.

The three types are as follows:

Modem Access

The modem is probably the most common means of allowing communication between remote computers. This is largely due to the modem's ability to use the public telephone system to transmit and receive digital information. The term 'Modem' refers to a process known as 'Modulate / Demodulate' and is simply a cutdown means of expressing a conversion process.

Using the modem to connect to the Internet requires a connection through the public telephone network. This means that the connection needs to be set up by a dial-up process similar to that used when dialling a telephone number in the usual way.

A modem can normally only be used to connect a single computer to another single remote computer. Software does exist that enables many computers to access a modem connected to a single PC over a network, but this is not a very elegant solution and generally requires some fairly complex setting up.

The main advantage of using a modem connection to connect to the Internet is that of a relatively low cost, both in terms of hardware and connection charges. Most Internet Service Providers(ISP) are now able to supply Internet access via a local number.

The disadvantages of using a modem connection are those of limited speed; of delays in connecting due to the time required to dial-up the connection number and the ability to only provide a one-to-one connection.

ISDN

ISDN is short for Integrated Services Digital Network. It was developed to overcome the shortcomings of the standard public telephone system when used to connect remote computers together. Essentially ISDN provides the means to allow digital communication to occur directly without first having to be converted (modulated/ demodulated) to the type of signal normally associated with the Public telephone system; hence the 'Digital Network'.

ISDN network have gradually evolved over recent years to encompass most of the developed world and are being used extensively by multinational corporations to transfer large amounts of data across continents and to provide 'real-time' multi-channel video-audio conferencing facilities.

There are 2 types of ISDN hardware available for connecting to the Internet.

ISDN – Single User Access

It allows ISDN connection from a single PC and is known as an ISDN Terminal Adapter. This kind of Internet access is most suitable for a single PC user who requires either a high speed connection or rapid access times. ISDN Terminal Adapters are available either as external devices that connect to the PC via a cable interface, or as internal PC cards.

ISDN – Multiple User Access

It is known as an ISDN Router and allows access for many PCs on a network to ISDN services. The ISDN Router is connected to the LAN in the same way that a PC is connected and simply behaves as an additional shared network resource.

An ISDN Router is so called because it has the capability to identify the destination address of incoming TCP/IP packets and assign the appropriate Ethernet addresses. The TCP/IP packets can then be delivered directly to the appropriate PC over the Ethernet LAN. This also means that many PCs can effectively share the ISDN resource so that multiple PC users on the same LAN can appear to access the Internet simultaneously.

Types of Modem

The types of modem that are available for PC users can broadly be defined as the following:

- Internal or External Modems
- Modems with or without Fax capabilities
- Modems with different data speed capabilities.

Difference between External & Internal Modems

An internal modem is fitted into one of the internal card slots within your PC. Internal modems can be of various types of depending on the type of PC architecture that your system contains.

External modems are those that connect to the PC via an interface cable, usually to one of the Serial Communications Ports available on your PC.

External modems hold an advantage over internal modems in that they normally display a range of status indicator lights, which can make the process of troubleshooting errors easier. More recently the process of modem configuration has been largely automated and so the need for this kind of information has diminished. The fact that external modems also need their own power supply means an increased cost and so in most cases the benefits of an external modem have been outweighed in favour of internal ones.

Both types are generally fitted with an internal speaker so that you can choose to monitor the sounds associated with the process of establishing a dial-up connection.

Fax Modems

Most of the popularly available modems include the capability to send and receive fax communications. The necessary software needed to implement this capability on your PC is often also provided in a rather primitive form. The main disadvantage of using a PC based

Fax system is that your PC must be switched on with the fax software running in order to receive faxes.

Speeds of Modems

The speed capabilities of a modem are indicated by its 'baud' rate. This term refers to the number of signal changes that occur per second at the output of the modem and is used as a measure of 'raw' output speed. The amount of actual data or 'bits' per second (bps) depends on the type and actual data or 'bits' per second (bps) depends on the type and degree of signal encoding that occurs and so the baud rate does not always indicate the true data rate. However, it is true to say that the higher the baud rate, the higher the theoretical data rate. In many cases the data rate of a modem is now quoted in 'bps' to avoid this confusion.

Until recently it was common to find modems available as either 9600 baud of 14400 baud. Now, with advances in modems technology it is more common to find modems available as 28800 or 33600 bps. More recently still, modems with speeds up to 56 Kbs are now available.

Modem Installation

Here we will concentrate on the installation of the internal modem, since external are relatively rare. Before installing a modem, it may be necessary to select a series of 'jumper' settings on the modem card. This will depend on the specific modem that you are installing. Many vendors allow these settings to be made via the accompanying software, eliminating the need to set these manually on the modem card itself.

If this is the case then simply install the modem as indicated below. If these settings do need to be set manually, then follow the instructions in the manufacturer's instruction manual to do this. Often the 'jumpers' will be set to default settings at the factory.

These settings will define two main elements: the 'Com Port' setting and the 'Interrupt' (or IRQ) setting. The important thing about these settings is that they must be unique to the modem. The processor uses the combination of these settings to communicate with the modem. All of the devices attached to your PC, such as the mouse, CD ROM, or Sound card will already be using some of the available settings to communicate with the processor and it is important that you do not duplicate any settings that are used by other devices.

Configuration of the Modem

Once the modem has been installed in your PC, you can begin configuring Windows to use the modem. There are several ways in which you can approach this. If your modem is identified as a Windows 'Plug and Play' compatible device then you can get Windows to recognise and configure the modem more or less automatically. If you do not have the manufacturer's installation disk, then you can usually configure the modem using one of Windows 'standard' modem drivers appropriate to the speed of the modem. If you have the manufacturer's installation disk, then you can use this to supply the modem specific drivers to Windows, allowing you to fully utilise any specialised features that your modem can support. Many modem suppliers now supply installation software that will fully automate the whole process. If this is the case, try installing the modem using the manufacturer's disk and instruction manual in the first place.

The following procedure allows you to install a modem.

1. Click on Start menu, Settings submenu, Control Panel and then Add New Hardware.
2. The Add New Hardware Wizard will appear.
3. The first Wizard dialog box tells you that this will add new hardware to the system.
4. The next dialog box, tells you that the system will search for a new hardware automatically.

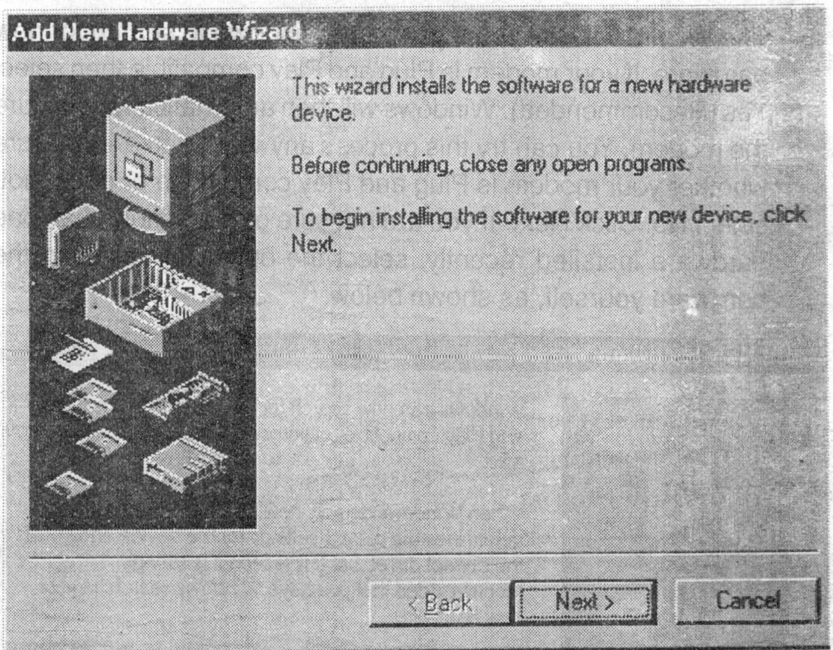
Add New Hardware Wizard
This wizard installs the software for a new hardware device.
Before continuing, close any open programs.
To begin installing the software for your new device, click Next.
< Back
Next >
Cancel

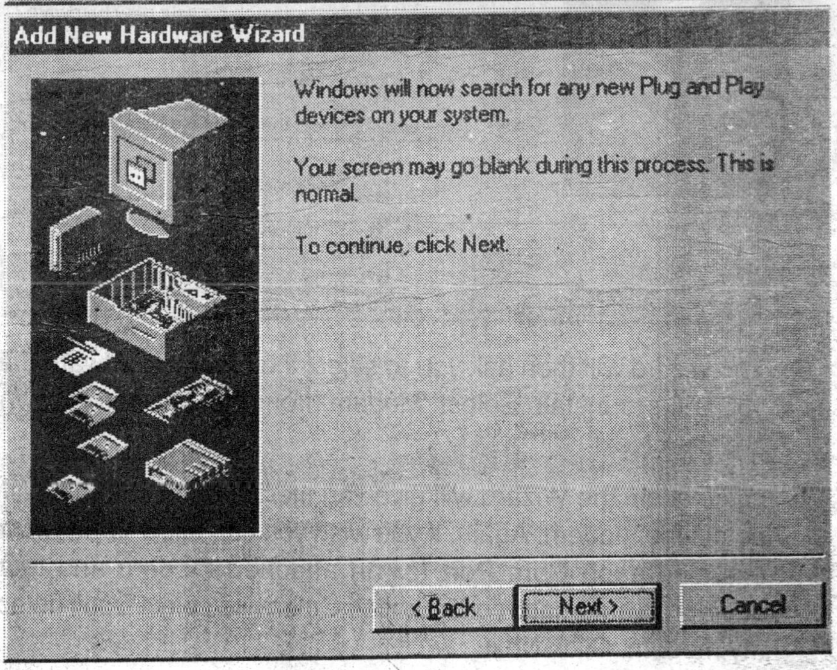
Add New Hardware Wizard
Windows will now search for any new Plug and Play devices on your system.
Your screen may go blank during this process. This is normal.
To continue, click Next.
< Back
Next >
Cancel

5. The Wizard will ask you if you want Windows to search for new hardware. If your modem is Plug and Play compatible then select Yes (Recommended). Windows will then automatically configure the modem. You can try this process anyway if you are not sure whether your modem is Plug and Play compatible or not. If not, select No. Click Next. If you are not sure or have more than one hardware installed recently, select the option of selecting the hardware yourself, as shown below.

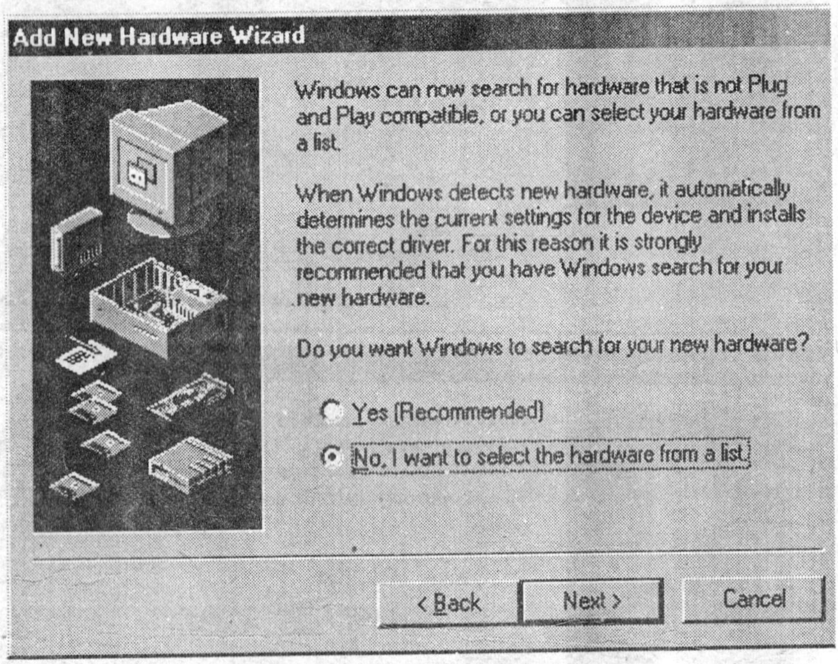

6. The wizard will then ask you to select the type of hardware that you wish to install. Select 'Modem' from the list (scroll down) and click Next.

7. Once again the Wizard will give you the option to automatically detect the modem. Again, if you wish you can allow Windows to examine each Com Port for an attached modem and then attempt an automatic configuration Otherwise select Don't detect my modem. Click Next.

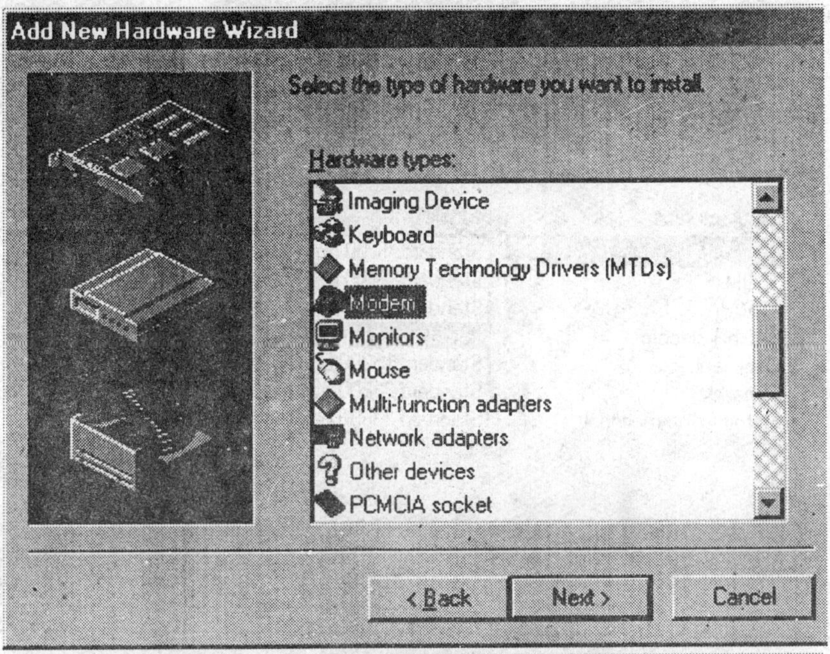
Add New Hardware Wizard
Select the type of hardware you want to install.
Hardware types:
Imaging Device
Keyboard
Memory Technology Drivers (MTDs)
Modem
Monitors
Mouse
Multi-function adapters
Network adapters
Other devices
PCMCIA socket
< Back
Next >
Cancel

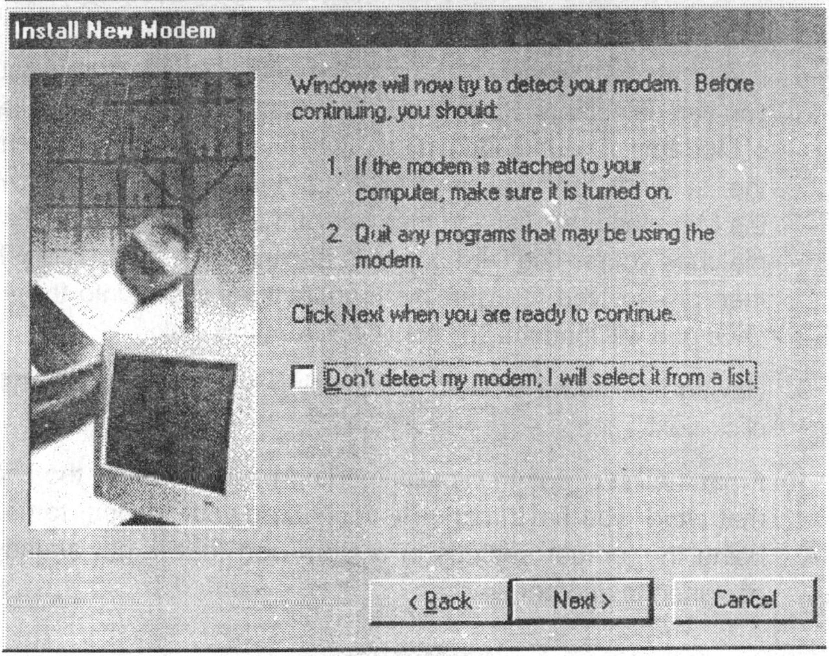
Install New Modem
Windows will now try to detect your modem. Before continuing, you should:
1. If the modem is attached to your computer, make sure it is turned on.
2. Quit any programs that may be using the modem.
Click Next when you are ready to continue.
Don't detect my modem; I will select it from a list.
< Back
Next >
Cancel

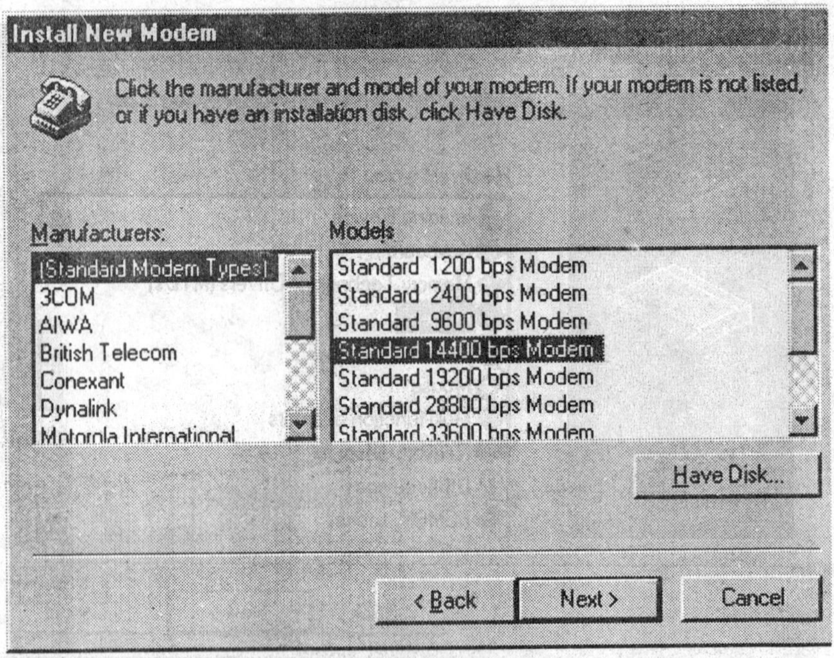

8. The Install New Modem window will appear.

   If your modem manufacturer is listed in the Manufacturers list, you can select this. Selecting a manufacturer will produce a list of Modems. If your modem model is available then select it from the list. If not, then you can select Standard Modem Types from the Manufacturers list and then select the sped of modem that matches yours. The third option is to click Have Disk. This will then prompt you to insert the manufacturer's disk into the A: drive and will load the correct driver from this disk.

9. Having selected a modem driver using one of these options, click Next.

10. From the list of communication ports presented, select the one that either you have manually configured your modem to use using the jumper settings or a Com port that is not already assigned to another device.

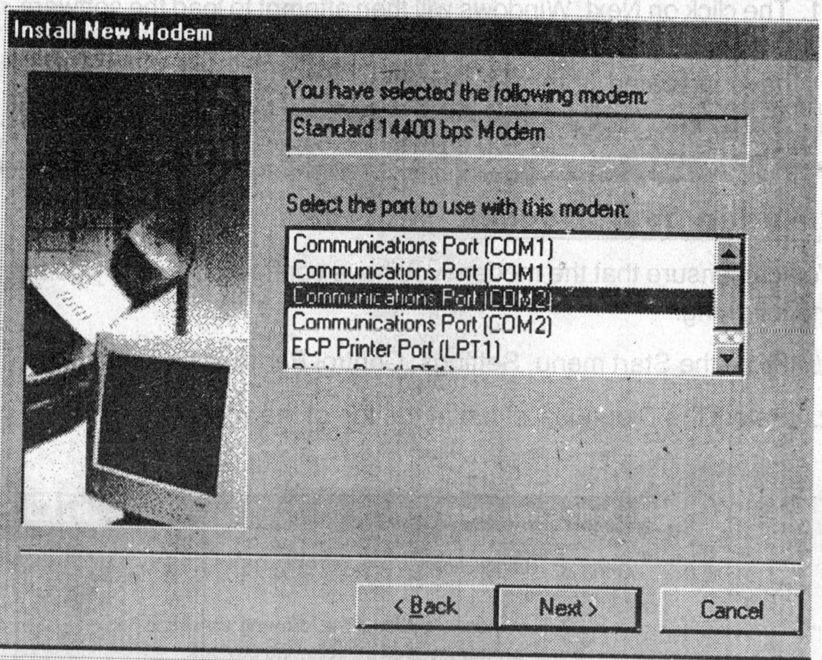
Install New Modem
You have selected the following modem:
Standard 14400 bps Modem
Select the port to use with this modem:
Communications Port (COM1)
Communications Port (COM1)
Communications Port (COM2)
Communications Port (COM2)
ECP Printer Port (LPT1)
< Back
Next >
Cancel

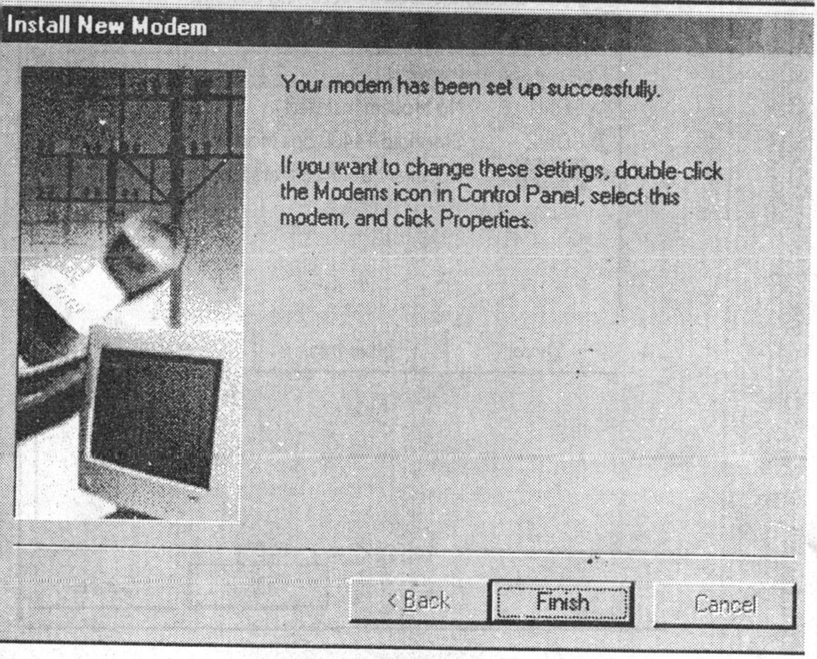
Install New Modem
Your modem has been set up successfully.
If you want to change these settings, double-click the Modems icon in Control Panel, select this modem, and click Properties.
< Back
Finish
Cancel

11. The click on Next. Windows will then attempt to load the software driver that you have selected and configure for the port that you have indicated. If this is successful, the wizard will report this and ask you to click Finish. You will then be returned to the Control Panel window.

Ensuring Your Modem

You can ensure that the modem you have configured is ok, by doing the following:

1. From the Start menu, Settings, Control Panel, click at Modems.
2. Select the Diagnostics' tab at the top of the window.

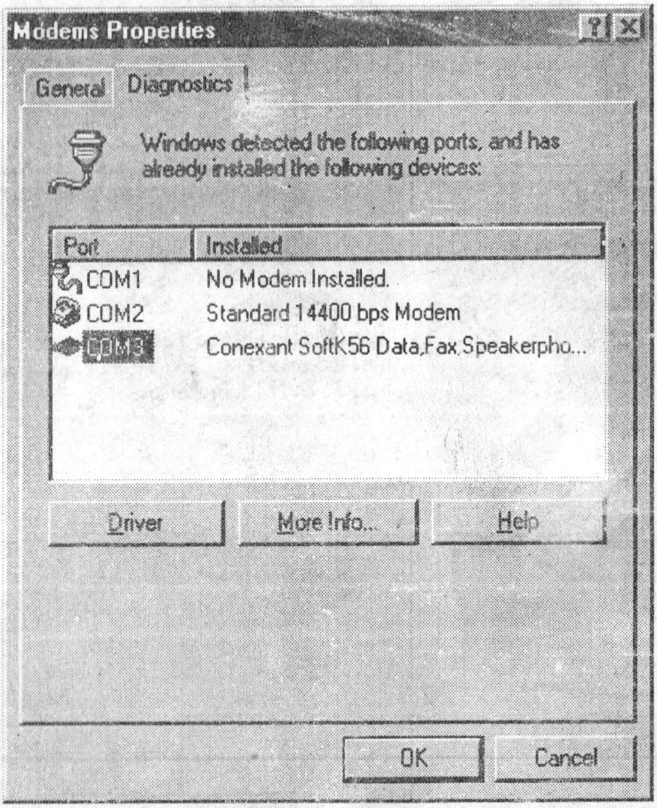

3. From the list of installed ports, select the one attached to the modem and then click More Info......

4. After a few seconds, during which Windows 98 sends a series of commands to the modem, a 'More Info........'. window will appear.

   This will show the complete details of the modem configuration together with all of the command results.

If the diagnostics test proceeds smoothly without reporting any errors, then your modem installation has been successful.

Otherwise you will need to check that the various modems settings are correct.

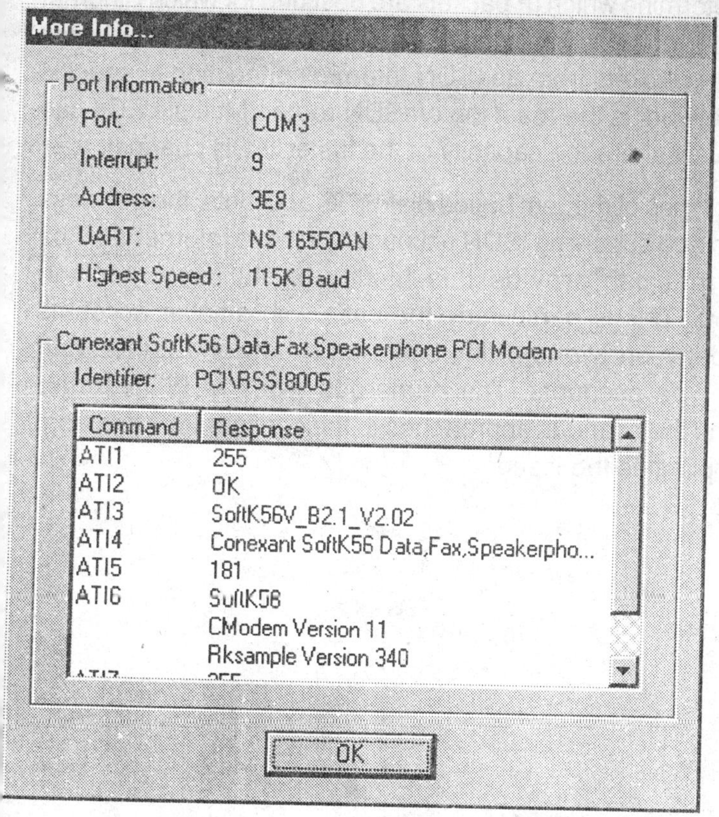

ISDN Hardware

There are two types of hardware that will allow ISDN access to the Internet. The first provides a service similar to the modem access in that it allows a single PC to connect to the Internet via an ISDN link. This type of connection requires an ISDN Terminal Adapter, which is usually installed as an internal PC card. It allows faster access than through a modem link, but is limited in that only PC can be connected (although software is available to extend this capability).

ISDN links can better be used to connect a number of PCs to the Internet at the same by 'routing' the connection via an ISDN Router. The ISDN router is connected on one port to the Internet and on another to an Ethernet network. The ISDN router then provides a means to determine which IP packets are destined for which Ethernet address and thereby to individual PCs on the network. This process of 'routing' IP packets from an ISDN Internet connection to specific PCs on a network is the main job of ISDN router. Multiple PCs can then effectively share the capacity of the faster ISDN channel.

Unlike most types of modem based dial-up IP accounts, the business of setting up and supplying ISDN accounts by those Internet Service Providers that can provide this facility is still very much in development. This is particularly the case with smaller accounts (aimed at between two and fifty users on a network) rather than 'corporate' type accounts. The numerous types of ISDN router available and their various approaches to the configuration process, further complicates the issue.

6

Getting Connected to Internet

Introduction

While connecting to Internet, various parties come into play. First you dial from your computer with the help of your telephone which has been provided by your local telephone company. From here the transmission goes to the satellite, this process is done by another party who is the service provider for this. Hence he is called Internet Service Provider. Now we will learn about this process in this chapter and how you would set your computers accordingly. But, first we would look at Internet Service Providers, which in India are very few like VSNL, Satyam Info, etc.

Internet Service Providers

It could be argued that, as the Internet Protocol is the single unifying feature of the Internet, the Internet is therefore IP and vice versa. Others might say that the Internet consists of all of the hardware infrastructure that connects all of the many thousands of computers together and provides the backbone of the Internet system.

The advantage user might simply say that the Internet is a service that can be derived from a number of different sources. Whatever your perspective, one definition that holds true is that for any resource to be a part of the Internet, it must be available to the rest of the Internet on a more or less continual basis.

Thus, any Internet resource must be quickly available on demand, if not actually 'hard wired' to the rest of the Internet. There is therefore a difference between the casual user of the Internet, i.e., someone who uses the Internet resource, and some person or organisation who supplies those resources.

In general terms it could be said that the casual user does not actually become a permanent part of the Internet, but merely 'dials-in' to the Internet on a temporary basis. The casual user therefore needs to be able to access an Internet 'access point' as required. The Internet Service Provides this access point either via a local public telephone number or via an ISDN link.

Those that provide more permanent links will effectively allow the end-user to become a true part of the Internet, and to provide Internet services. We can now turn to the various types of Internet Service Providers.

There are two basic types of service providers: those that provide a variety of purely Internet based services, which we will call Internet Access Providers, and those that provide other information services, which are known as Content Providers.

Internet Access Providers

The Internet Service Provider (ISP) offers means to provide a dial-up link via a publicly available telecommunication service, i.e., telephone or ISDN, which supports an IP channel across that link. The ISP then handles the IP packets coming from and going to that link. In order to support the IP link across the telephone system, an additional protocol is required, which an ISP must also be able to support. This will either be the Point-to-Point Protocol (PPP) or the Serial Line Internet Protocol (SLIP). As PPP has largely replaced SLIP access now, for the following configuration procedures we will assume PPP. The ISP must also provide a means of resolving what are known as 'Domain Name' address queries.

This process will be supplied by the ISP's 'domain Name Server'. The IP protocol provides a means of converting Domain Names, which people can understand, into IP addresses (eg, 012.345.678.9) which computers can understand. Thus when you type a URL into your web browser, the Domain Name part of the URL must first be converted into its IP address before the Web page can be located and delivered to the browser.

Each Domain Name is assigned its specific IP address when it is created and so the process of converting one to the other is simply a matter of looking up its entry in a database. Finding where that particular Domain Name/IP address relationship is recorded and then using this information to make the correct conversion is the job of the 'Domain Name Server' (DNS).

The minimum basic services that an ISP must provide can be summarised as follows:

- Dial-up access for either analogue (public telephone) or digital (ISDN) telecom links
- Support for the PPP protocol
- Support for handling IP packets
- Access to a Domain Name Server

As these are the basic minimum, most ISPs will provide these as a matter of course and will not necessarily advertise these capabilities.

E-MAIL SERVICES

Most of the ISPs also provide e-mail services. An 'E-mail Server' at the ISP will provide e-mail sending and collection capabilities, similar in effect to that provided by a normal mail Post Box. When you register with an ISP, an e-mail 'account' is set up on the mail server. You will then be able to send e-mail via the ISP using suitable e-mail 'client' software on your PC.

Any e-mail that is sent to your e-mail address(es) is collected by the mail server at the ISP, for delivery to you when you are ready. ISPs will normally provide you with one or more e-mail addresses, depending on the type of account that you select. Many will restrict the number of e-mail addresses that you can use, while a few allow an unlimited number of e-mail addresses. Having several e-mail addresses means that you could, for instance, allocate different addresses to members of your family; or in a small business environment, to members of staff. Several e-mail accounts will generally operate under a single Internet access account. Those ISPs that provide an unlimited number of e-mail account under a single Internet access account can represent a considerable saving if your organisational needs are for more than just a few e-mail accounts.

In these circumstances, consideration needs to be given as to how multiple e-mail addresses are collected and managed at the user end of the Internet link. Special e-mail software packages which act as local e-mail sorting agents are available. These act as a intermediaries between the ISPs Mail Sever and the individual users on a network and sort incoming e-mail so that e-mail addresses to different addresses is directed over the network to the appropriate e-mail client.

Configurating the Computer for Internet

Now that the selection part of the ISP is over, we are now ready to configure the modem to connect via the ISP to the Internet using the built-in Windows 98 Internet services. In more or less the same way, in order to configure the modem to be able to communicate with the modem equipment at the ISP and thus to the Internet, we need first to install and configure a modem adapter driver, (which for Windows 98 is known as the 'Dial-Up-Adapter'), and then to install and configure the network protocol (which in this case is TCP/IP).

TCP/IP protocol driver was installed the NetBEUI driver and so will only now need to configure this to work with the Dial-Up Adapter. These two setup procedures may appear rather technical, but once successfully set up, they will allow the day-to-day business of connecting to the Internet to proceed smoothly and easily and without having to be reconfigured, except perhaps if you choose to change your ISP. Once we have set up the adapter and protocol settings, we will then need to set up the Windows 98 Dial-Up Networking utility. This utility simply manages the dial-up process itself, allowing you to enter different dial-up profiles for dialling into different services.

Installing Dial Up Adapter

You will first need to check that the 'Dial-Up Networking facility was installed during the Windows 98 setup. From the Windows 98 Desktop view, double-click on 'My computer' and check for the presence of 'Dial-Up Networking'. If this is not present, then you will need to install it from your Windows 98 CD or setup disks as follows.

1. Click on Start Menu, Settings, Control Panel to show the Control Panel.
2. Double click on Add/Remove Programs and then click on the Windows 98 Setup tab.

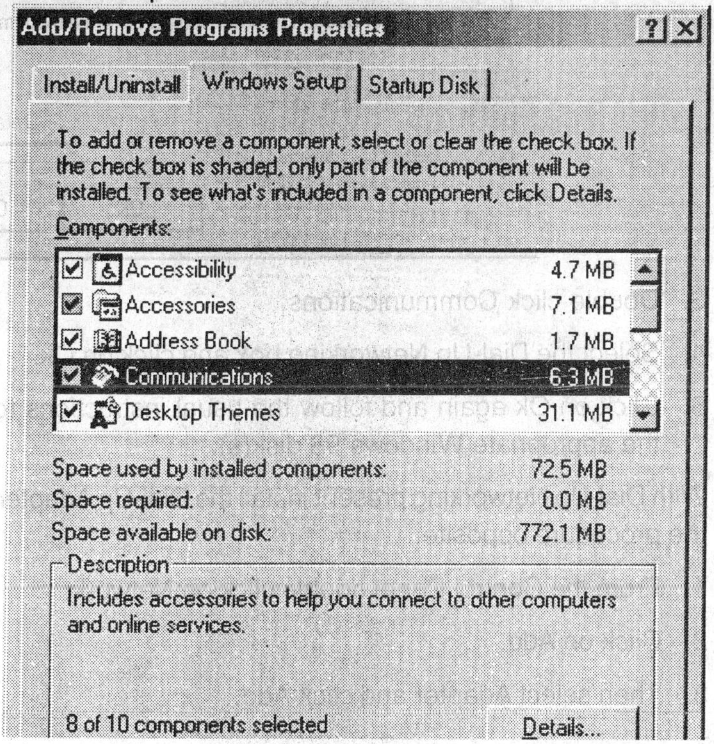

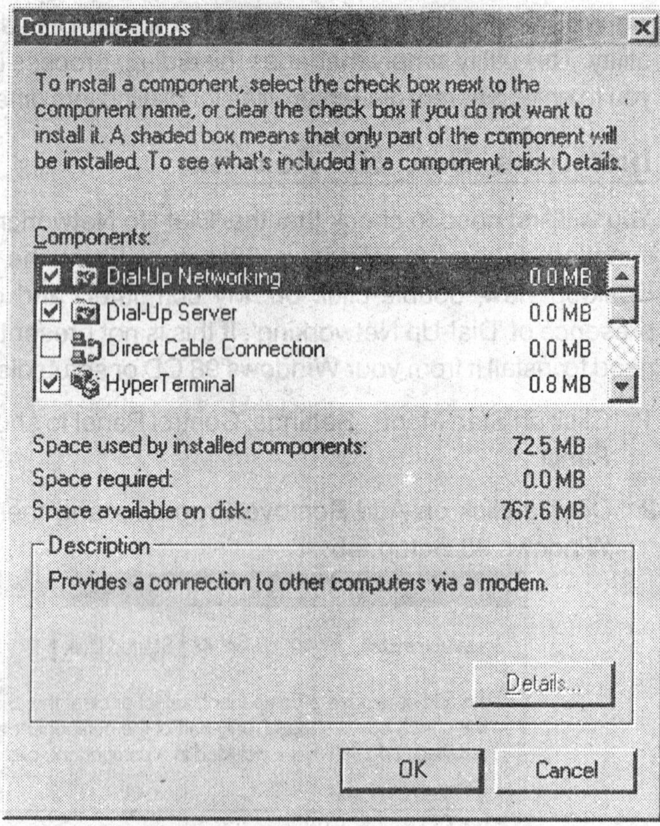

3. Double click Communications.
4. Select the Dial-Up Networking box and click on Ok.
5. Click on Ok again and follow the usual instructions for loading the appropriate Windows 98 disk(s).

With Dial-Up Networking present install the Dial-Up Adapter following the procedure opposite:

1. From the Control Panel double click on Network.
2. Click on Add.
3. Then select Adapter and click Add.

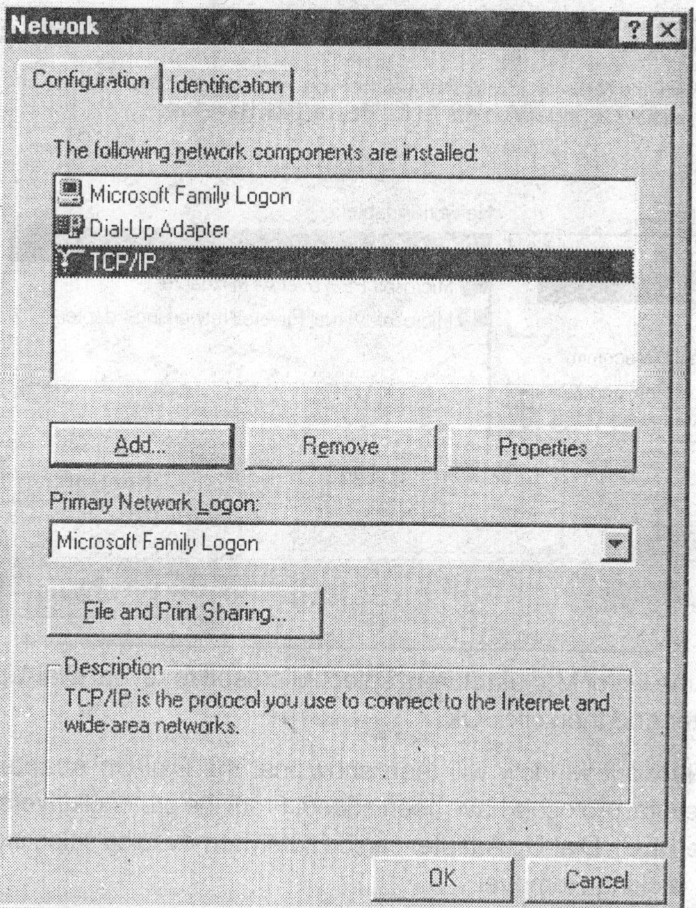
Network
Configuration
Identification
The following network components are installed:
Microsoft Family Logon
Dial-Up Adapter
TCP/IP
Add...
Remove
Properties
Primary Network Logon:
Microsoft Family Logon
File and Print Sharing...
Description
TCP/IP is the protocol you use to connect to the Internet and wide-area networks.
OK
Cancel

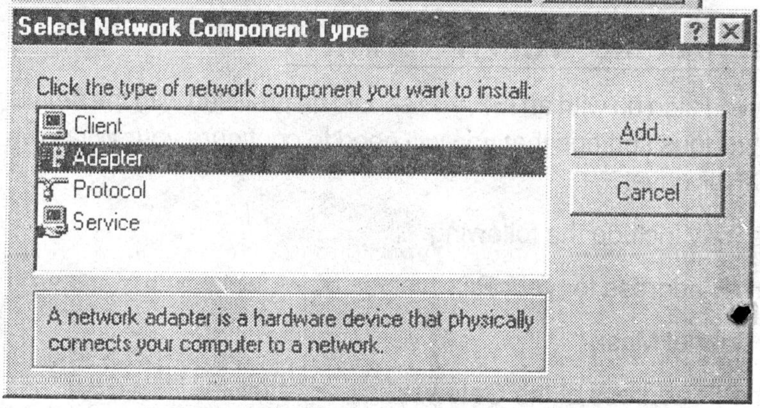
Select Network Component Type
Click the type of network component you want to install:
Client
Adapter
Protocol
Service
Add...
Cancel
A network adapter is a hardware device that physically connects your computer to a network.

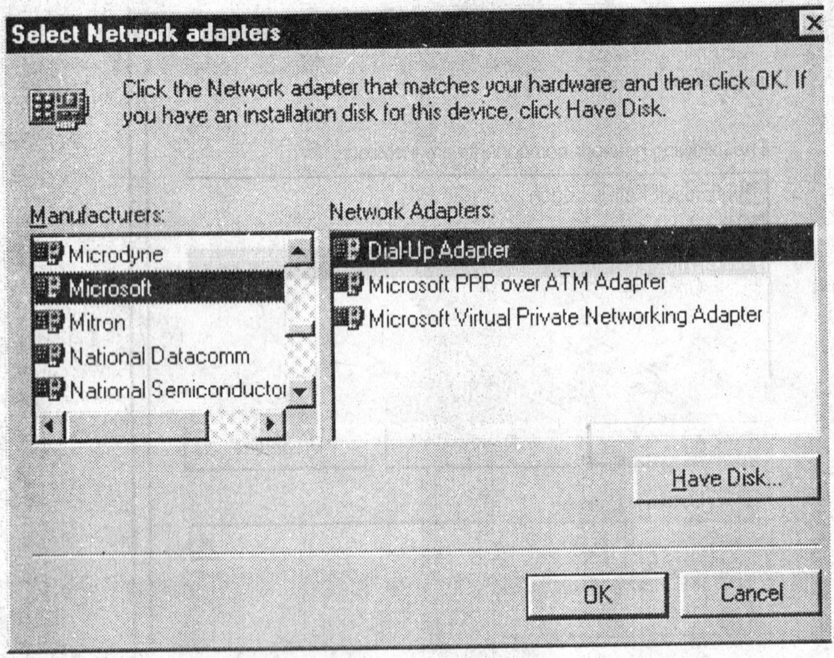

4. From the list of Manufacturers select Microsoft to reveal Dial-Up Adapter and then click Ok.
5. The Network window will then show that the Dial-Up Adapter and several protocols have been added. From the protocol drivers, the NetBEUI, Dial-Up Adapter can be safely removed by selecting it and clicking Remove.

Configurating TCP/IP Services

When you sign up with an ISP, you should be provided with the details of the various settings that you will need to configure your Windows 98 TCP/IP driver.

These may include the following:

- An IP address for your PC.
- A Subnet Mask
- The IP address of the Gateway

- A Host name, sometimes also called the username
- A Domain name
- The IP address(es) of the Domain Name Server.

In case any of these information is not available you can call your ISP support line to get these details, which may be referred to in a slightly different manner, but these are the terms which Windows 98 uses for TCP/IP configuration. Some ISPs will dynamically allocate an IP address to each new connection. In this case some of the following settings will differ slightly, as explained in the steps.

To configure your TCP/IP driver, proceed as follows.

1. From the Control Panel double-click on Network.
2. From the list of installed network components, select the TCP/IP, Dial-Up Adapter.

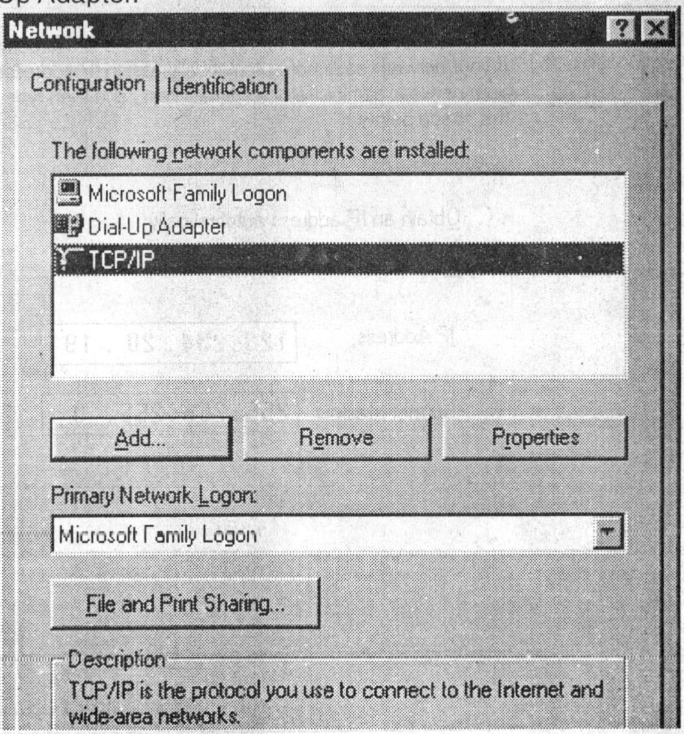

3. Click on Properties and then click on Ok at the TCP/IP Properties Information dialogue.
4. You will then be presented with the TCP/IP Properties window. Select the IP Address tab at the top, if this is not already selected.
5. If your ISP allocates IP addresses dynamically, select Obtain IP address automatically and skip above 2 steps. Otherwise select the Specify an iP Address button.
6. Enter the IP Address that has been allocated to your PC.
7. Enter the Subnet Mask (usually 255.255.255.0).

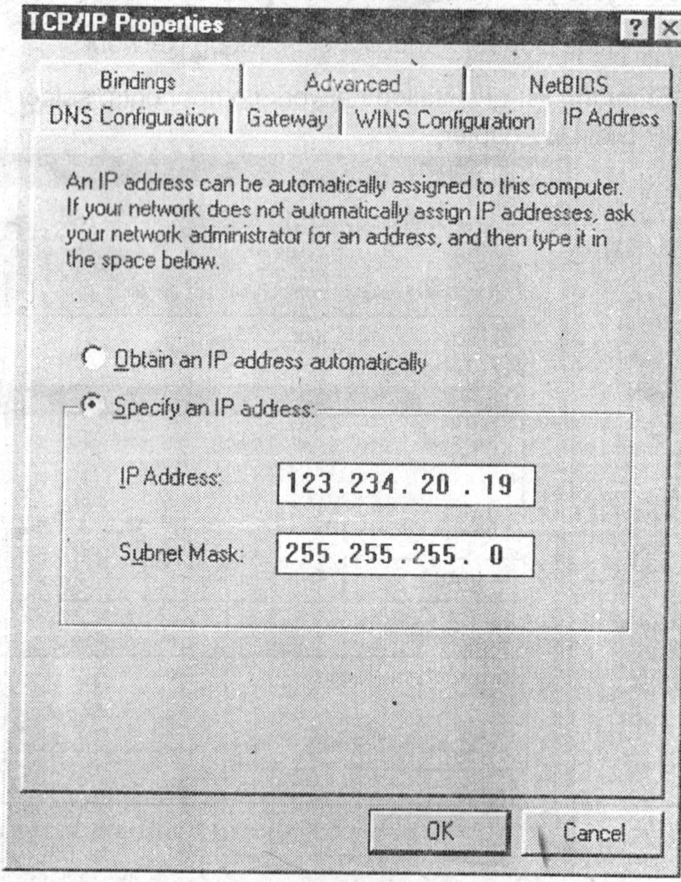

The details entered in the example above are for illustration only.

To continue, select the 'Gateway' tab at the top of the window

1. Enter the 'Gateway' IP address.
2. Click 'Add'.

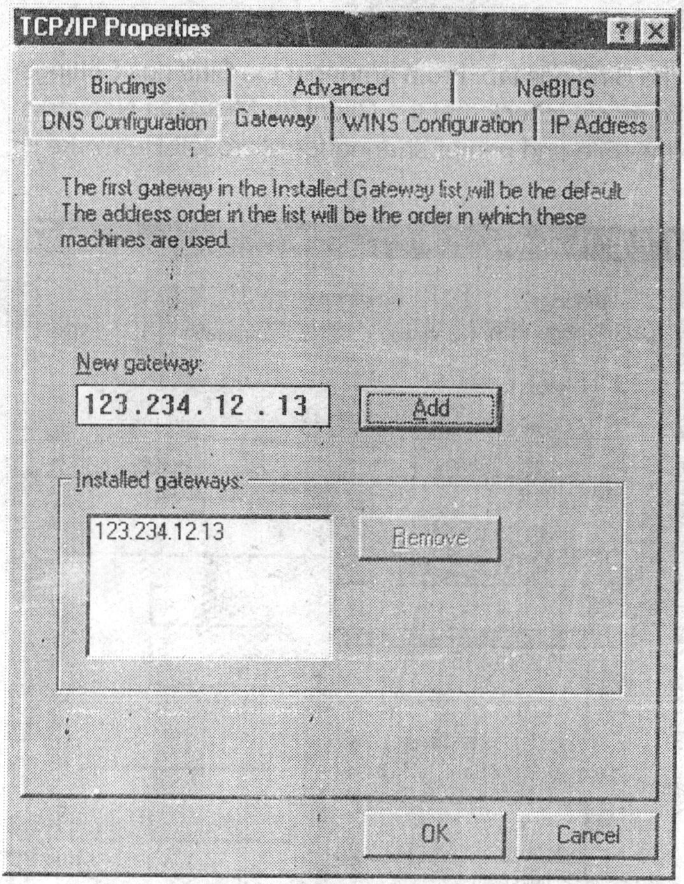

Next, select the DNS Configuration tab.

1. Select the Enable DNS button.
2. Enter the Host name.
3. Enter the Domain name.

4. Enter the 'Domain Name Server' IP address.
5. Click on 'Add'.
6. Enter the 'Domain Name' again here.
7. Click on 'Add' here.

Beware: Host and Domain name entries may be case sensitive.

Now click on the Bindings tab. From amongst the Bindings Settings (You may have more), check that the Client for Microsoft Networks is ticked and the 'File and printer sharing for Microsoft Networks is not.

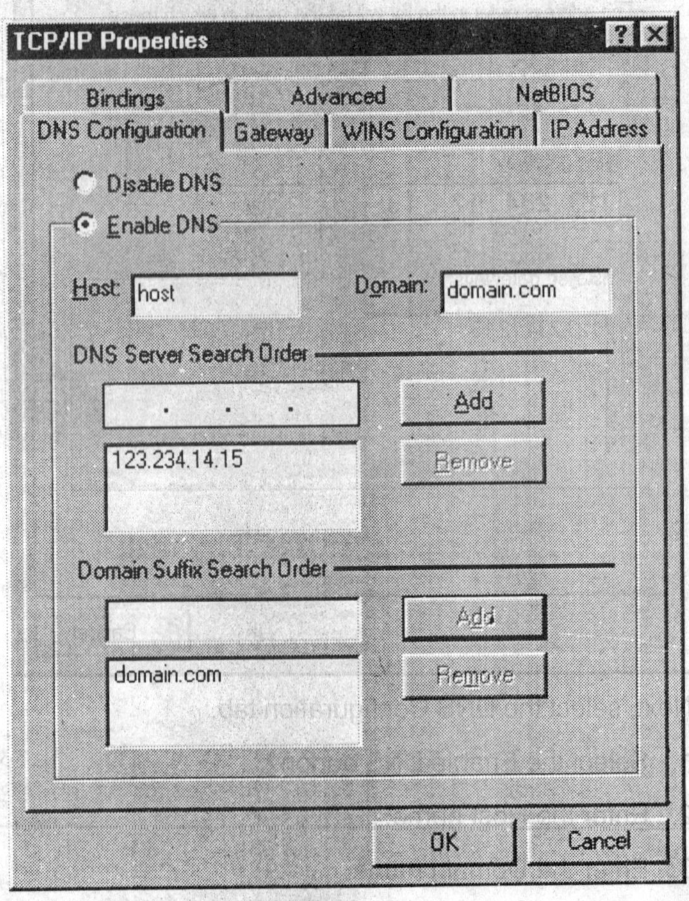

1. Tick Client for Microsoft Networks.
2. Un-tick File and printer sharing for Microsoft Networks.

Setting up Dial-Up Networking

Now that we have set up the adapter and protocol drivers, we need to define a 'Dial-up Networking' connection profile for the ISP. This utility allows you to specify the local access telephone number as allocated by your ISP and to set up the modem for that particular connection.

To configure this utility, proceed as follows:

1. Minimize or close all of the current active Windows 98 windows until you are left with the Desktop view.
2. Double-click on My Computer.
3. Double-click on Dial-Up Networking.

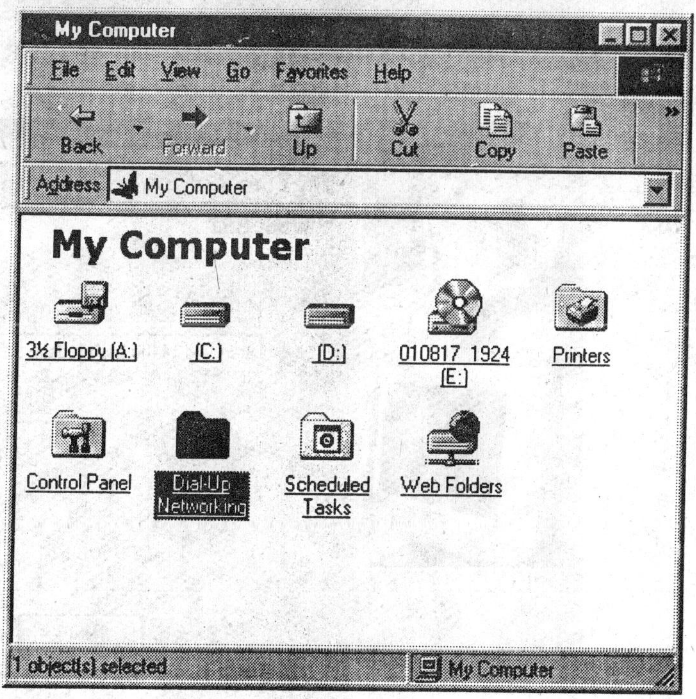

4. Double-click on Make New Connection. This will reveal the Make New Connection wizard as follows.

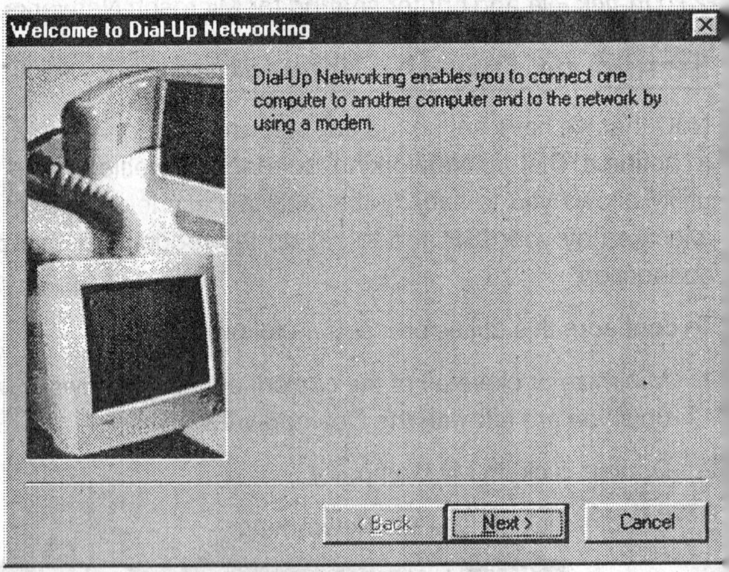

5. Type over the My Connection default with any text to describe your ISP connection profile, e.g., ISP.

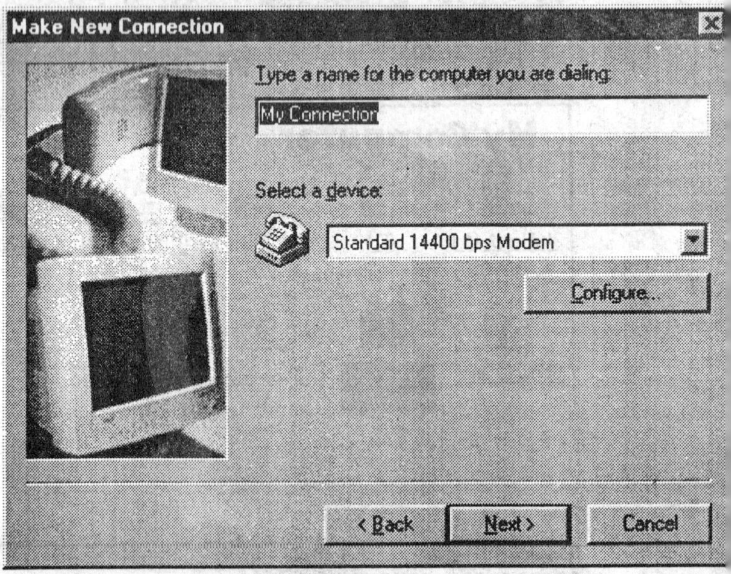

6. Your installed modem(s) will be displayed in the Select a modem drop-down menu (my modem is displayed). If you have more than one modem installed, then select the one that you wish to use to connect to your ISP. Otherwise, click Next.

7. Enter the Area Code and Telephone number of your ISP access number.

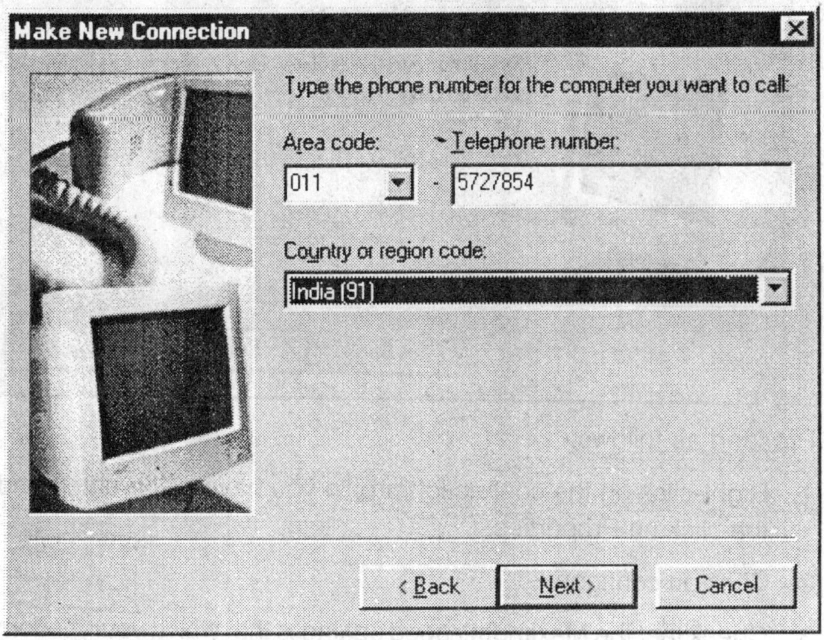

8. Select the country in which you are located form the drop-down menu.

9. Click on Next and then Finish. Your new connection profile will now be displayed in the Dial-up Networking window.

Having defined a new connection profile, we must now configure the modem and ISP server settings. The modem settings required for your ISP connection may differ from those given below in some respects, but in most cases the settings given should work. If not, then consult your ISP for the appropriate modem settings.

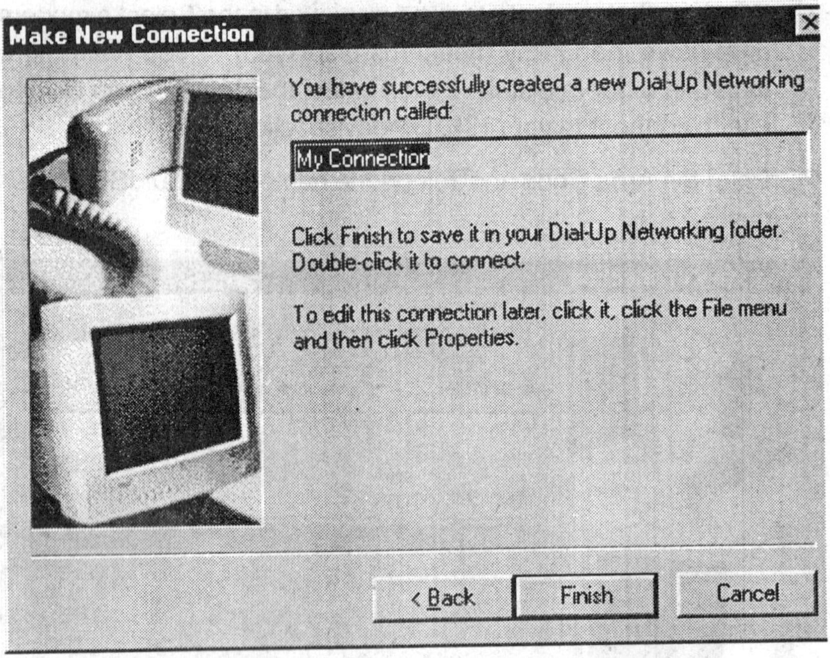

Proceed as follows:

1. Right-click on the connection profile you have just created and the click on Properties.
2. Click on configure.
3. Check that the Maximum speed setting is that which your modem will support, or if appropriate, as recommended by your ISP.
4. Click on the Connection tab.
5. Check that the modem settings are as indicated, or set according to your ISP.
6. Activate the Disconnect a call if idle.... tick-box and set an appropriate time. Then click on Advanced.
7. If your modem will support Error control and Compression (most likely) then ensure that the Use error control tick-box is activated, along with the Compress data tick-box.

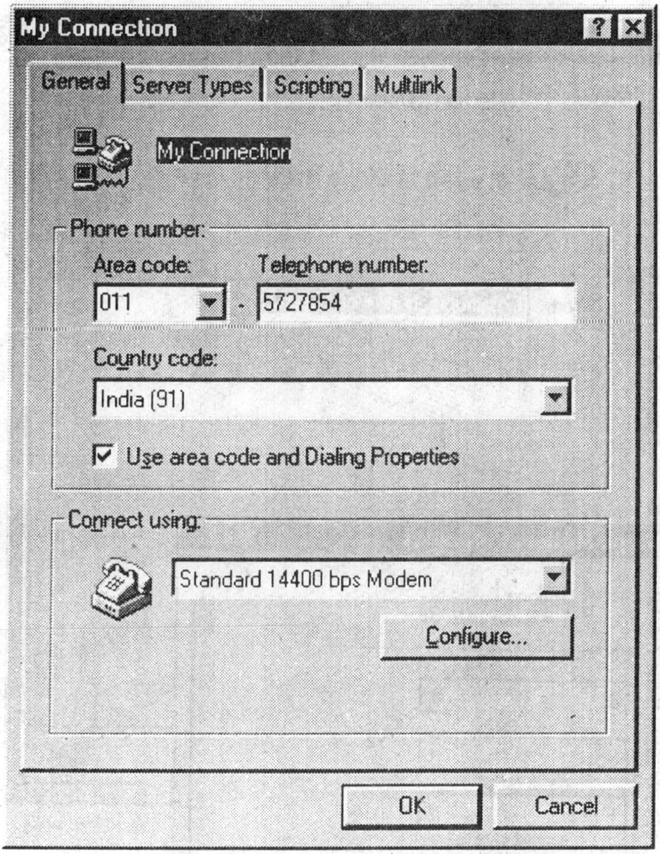

8. Ensure that Use Flow control is activated. If using an internal modem, then select Hardware (RTS/CTS). If you are using an external modem, then you may need to select Software (XON/XOFF).

9. If Modulation type is required (not required in this case), select Standard. Click on Ok.

You will be returned to the Modern Properties window. Now click on the Options' tab.

1. Activate the Bring up terminal window after dialling tick-box.

2. Click on Ok

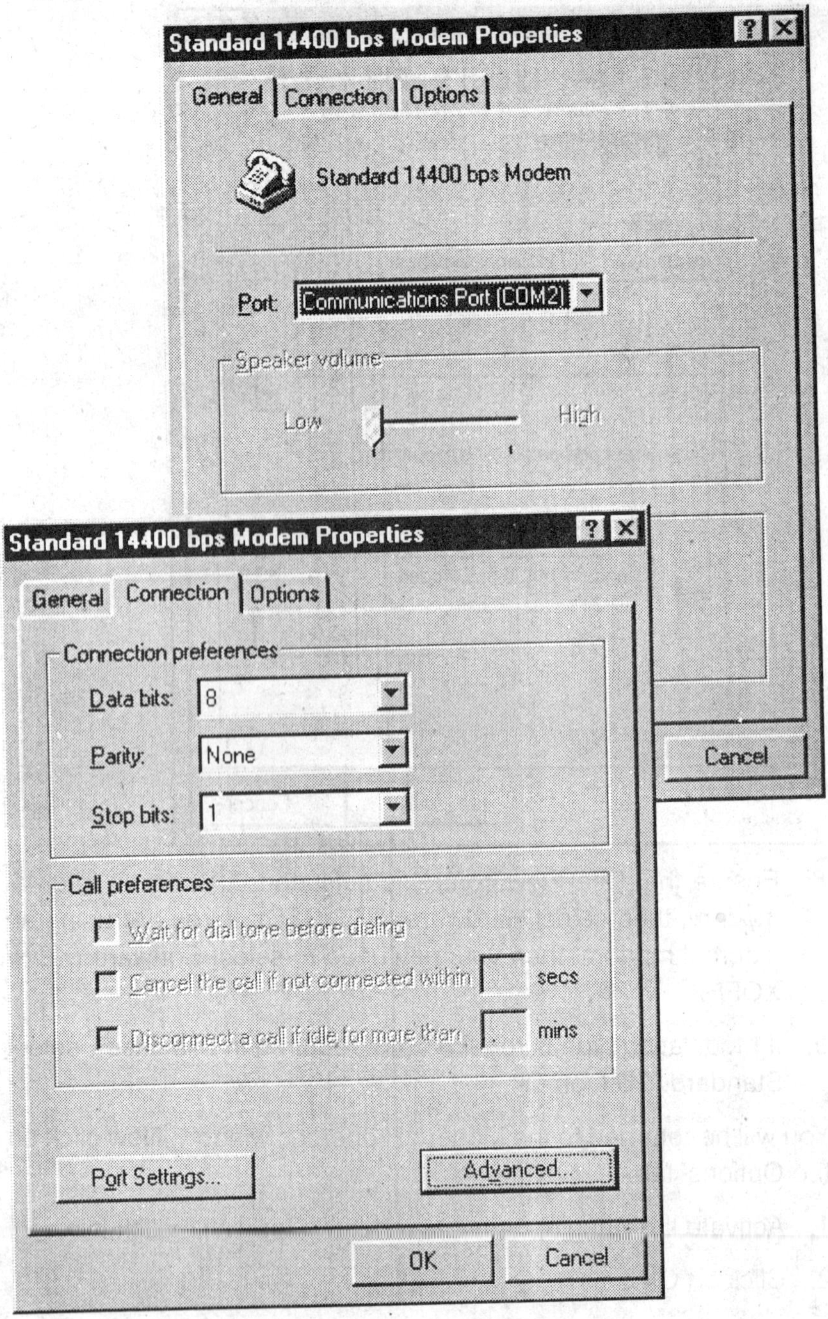
Standard 14400 bps Modem Properties
General
Connection
Options
Standard 14400 bps Modem
Port: Communications Port (COM2)
Speaker volume
Low
High
Cancel
Standard 14400 bps Modem Properties
General
Connection
Options
Connection preferences
Data bits: 8
Parity: None
Stop bits: 1
Call preferences
Wait for dial tone before dialing
Cancel the call if not connected within
secs
Disconnect a call if idle for more than
mins
Port Settings...
Advanced...
OK
Cancel

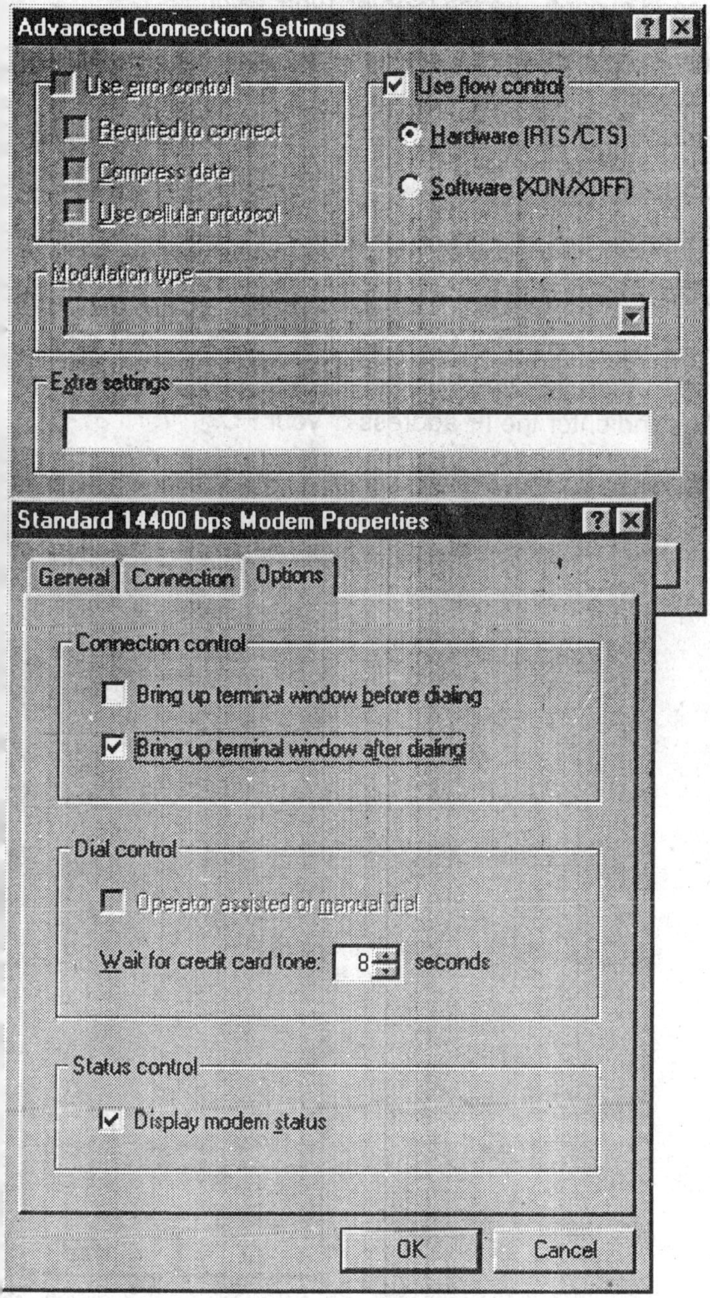
Advanced Connection Settings
Use error control
Required to connect
Compress data
Use cellular protocol
Use flow control
Hardware (RTS/CTS)
Software (XON/XOFF)
Modulation type
Extra settings
Standard 14400 bps Modem Properties
General
Connection
Options
Connection control
Bring up terminal window before dialing
Bring up terminal window after dialing
Dial control
Operator assisted or manual dial
Wait for credit card tone: 8 seconds
Status control
Display modem status
OK
Cancel

Finally, we need to configure the 'Server Type' settings.

1. From the Properties window as in the previous Step 2, click on Server Types.
2. Select PPP: Internet, Windows NT server, Windows 98.... from the drop-down menu.
3. Ensure that the only box ticked is TCP/IP.
4. Click on TCP/IP Settings....
5. If your ISP allocates IP addresses dynamically, select Server assigned IP address. Otherwise select the Specify an IP address checkbox and enter the IP address of your PC.

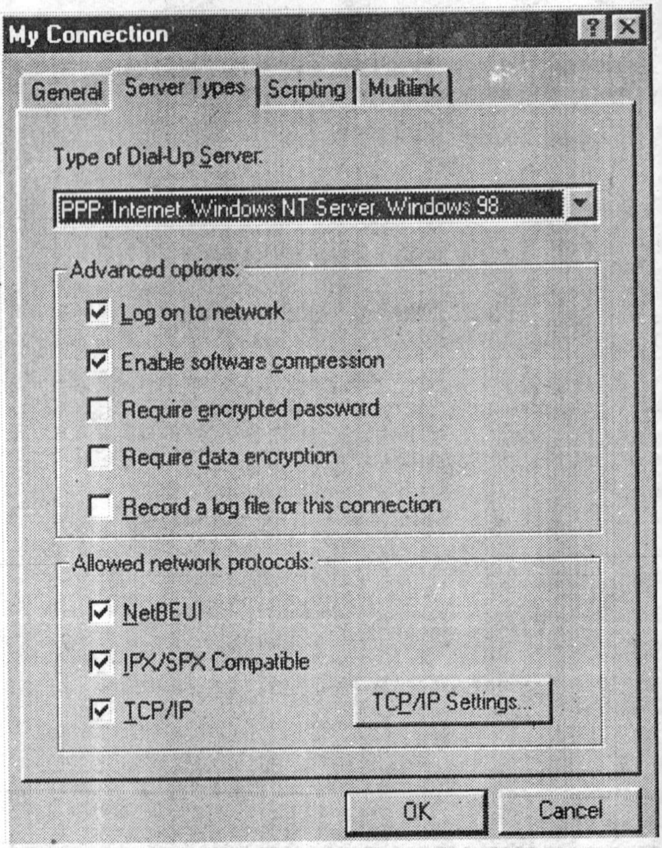

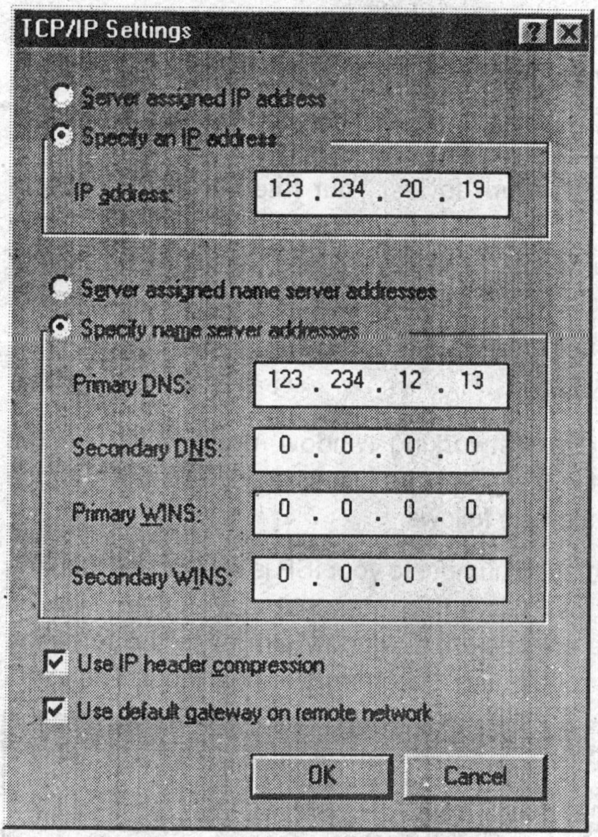

6. Activate the 'Specify name server addresses' checkbox and enter the IP address(es) of the Domain Name Server (DNS) in the Primary DNS location and the Secondary DNS if appropriate.
7. Leave the 'Use IP header compression' and 'Use default gateway on remote network' ticked and click on 'OK' in the TCP/IP Setting', 'Server Types' and the main 'Properties' window.

Connecting Modem

Now that we have completed the somewhat laborious process of setting up your modem Internet access, you should now be able to successfully connect to the Internet.

To connect to your ISP manually, you will need your Host account name and password as well as your IP address.

Manual Dial-Up Setting

We will use this procedure to test your Internet access before proceeding to the automatic dial-up configuration. Your ISP will have supplied you with a username which may well be the same as your Host name and a password to allow access to your Internet account. You will also need your IP address,

For this do the following:

1. From the Dial-Up Networking window, double-click on the connection profile that you have just created. This will start the Connect To window as follows.
2. Check that the dial-up number to your ISP is correct and ignoring any Username or Password entries that may appear, click on Connect. Once connected, a window similar to the following should appear, requesting a username or host input. The exact

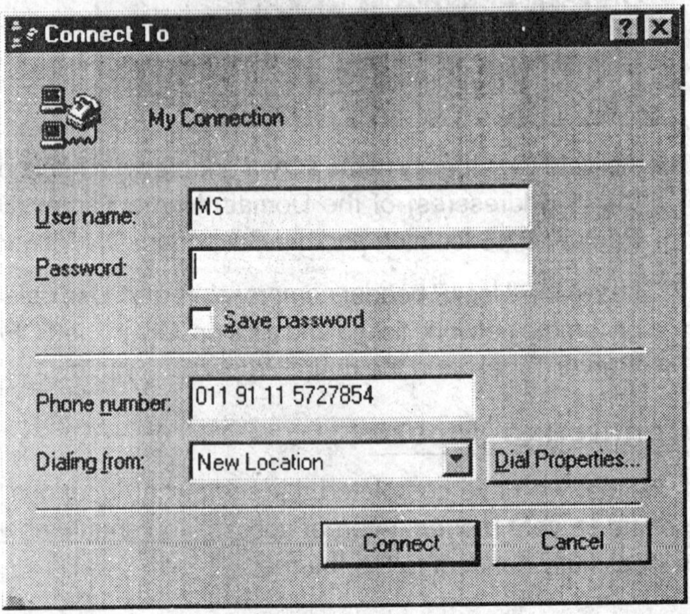

text may differ for different ISPs. If it does not appear, or if the output text is garbled, you may need to examine or reset your modem settings.

3. Enter your username being careful to use the correct type case (Capitalisation or lower case) and press the Enter key.

4. You will then be prompted to enter a password. Type this in for security reasons it may not appear on screen, so type carefully and press Enter. If this is accepted, then command prompt will appear.

5. At the command prompt, type ppp, then a space, and then your IP address. Again, type this carefully as any mistakes are unlikely to be correctable, except by starting the dial-up process from scratch.

6. Press the Enter key. You should now see a response form the ISP giving details of your PPP connection, followed by a string of garbled characters. When this occurs, click on Continue or press the F7 key.

You should now see this.... followed after a short delay by a Logging on dialogue and then a Connection Established window. If so...... Congratulations! You are now connected to the internet! Disconnect by clicking on the connected icon in the Windows 98 control bar and then clicking on Disconnect.

Sharing a Fax Modem

In the same way it is possible to share printer and directory/file resources over a network, it is also possible to share a fax modem that is installed on one of the networked PCs. This facility is not, however, a standard part of the Windows 98 system setup and requires the installation of some specialised files form the Windows 98 CD. The specific files required will depend on our existing Windows 98 setup.

To setup fax sharing you will certainly need to install a fax enabling file from the Windows 98 CD. If you do not have either Windows Messaging, Microsoft Exchange client, or Microsoft Outlook (all MAPI clients) installed on the PCs that will need access to the shared fax service, you will also need access to the shared fax service, you will also need to install the Windows Messaging installation file onto each PC before installing the fax enabling file.

In outlining the fax sharing configuration, I will assume that you have none of the above installed. If you do have any of the three programs mentioned above installed, then you can skip the next section.

Installing Windows Messaging

1. Insert the Windows 98 CD, double-click on the tools/oldwin95/message/intl/wms.exe file and click Yes to Are you sure... and then Yes again.
2. Select Yes to the question Have you used Windows Messaging before. Click Next.
3. De-select the Microsoft Mail entry and then select the Manually configure information services option. Click Next.
4. Enter Fax into the Profile Name dialogue. Click Next and then Ok in the Fax Properties window.
5. Click on Finish.

Installing the Fax enabling software

1. Insert the Windows 98 CD, double-click on the tools/oldwin95/message/intl/awfax.exe file and then click Yes (provided you are sure that the conditions are fulfilled).
2. Click on Yes to restart your computer.

Once you have installed both the fax enabling software and at least one of the above MAPI clients onto each of the PCs that will be sharing the fax service.

Making the Fax Modem available........

1. On the fax modem PC, start the MAPI client (Windows Messaging/Inbox or Outlook, etc) from the desktop and select the Fax profile that we created earlier. Click on Ok.
2. Click on Tools, Services from the toolbar.
3. Click on Add, select Microsoft Fax from the options and click on Ok.
4. You will be asked to specify certain details.... click on Yes and enter your return Fax number as a minimum. Click on Ok.
5. Click on Yes to specify a fax modem. Select the Let other people.... option and click on Ok to select the default hard drive.
6. If you only have one fax modem installed, then this will already be selected. Otherwise, choose form the list. Click on Ok, Ok again and Ok once more to finish the configuration. Now restart the MAPI client and leave it running.

Configuring shared fax resource access....

1. From the PCs requiring the shared fax access, start the MAPI client (Windows Messaging/Inbox or Outlook, etc) from the desktop and click on New in the Choose a Profile window.
2. Select only the Microsoft Fax service, de-selecting any other options and click on Next.
3. Enter Fax as the Profile Name and click on Next.
4. Click on Add as if to add a new fax modem, select Network fax server and click on Ok.
5. Enter the Path in the form \\host\fax where host is the name of the PC that has the shared fax resource. Then select this new entry and click on Next.
6. Fill out the name and fax number details as required and click on Next.

7. Replace mailbox.pab with fax.pab and click on Next, then replace mailbox.pst with fax.pst and click on Next. Click on Finish, then Ok, and then restart the PC.

You should now be able to send documents from your Microsoft word processing programs.

Automatic Dial-Up

Having established that your Internet dial-up connection is working correctly, we can now automate the process so that your username, password and IP address are passed to the ISP without you having to type then in every time.

This is done by defining a Dial-Up Script, which is simply a set of text containing these parameters and which is processed when you initiate the modem dial-up.

Your ISP may be able to supply you with a script file that will be suitable for your particular type of connection. If your ISP can supply you with a suitable script (this will be a file with an '.scp suffix), then copy it now into the C:/ Program Files/Accessories' directory. If not, then you will need to edit your own script.

The script outlined below is intended as a guide only and may not work for your particular ISP without further modification. To produce this sample script, proceed as follows:

1. Click on Start Menu, Programs, Accessories, then click on Notepad. This will open the simple Windows 98 text editor with a blank page.
2. Copy out the following text, using the tab keys where necessary so that the text is laid out as shown. Insert your own username, password and IP address is indicated.

```
proc main
    delay 3
    waitfor "name"
```

```
    transmit "username"
    transmit "M"
    waitfor "password"
    transmit "M"
    waitfor "xxxx>"
    transmit "PPP 123.345.456.789"
    transmit "M"
endproc
```

Replace 'username' with your own username. Do not omit the quotation marks. Replace 'password with your own password. Replace the 'xxxx>, with exactly the text that appeared as the 'command prompt' when you used the manual dial-up method. Replace the '123.345.456.789' with your own IP address. Do not omit the 'PPP' (remember the space) or the quotation marks.

3. When completed, click on 'File' and 'Save As' and save the file as 'isp.scp' in the C:\Program\Files\Accessories\' directory as above.

To install your script, proceed as follows:

1. From the 'Desktop' view (i.e., minimize all current windows), double-click on 'My Computer'. Then double-click on 'Dial-Up Networking'.
2. Right-click on the ISP connection profile that you created in 'Dial-Up Networking Configuration' and then click on 'Properties'. This will bring up the 'General' Properties of this connection profile as follows:
3. Click on the 'Scripting' tab.
4. Click on the 'Browse button.
5. Select the appropriate script file and then click on 'Open'.
6. The script file and path now appears in the 'File name' entry. Click on 'OK'.

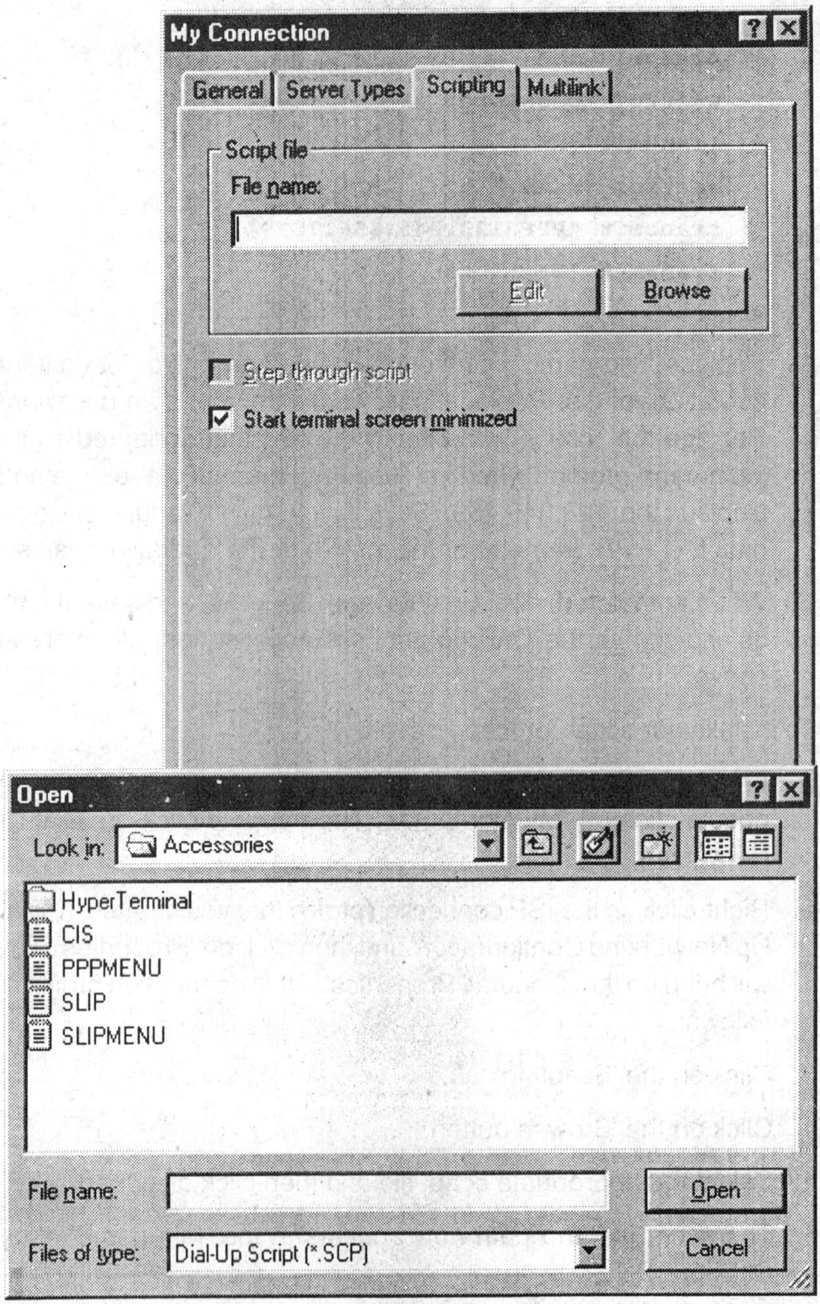
My Connection
General
Server Types
Scripting
Multilink
Script file
File name:
Edit
Browse
Step through script
Start terminal screen minimized
Open
Look in:
Accessories
HyperTerminal
CIS
PPPMENU
SLIP
SLIPMENU
File name:
Files of type:
Dial-Up Script (*.SCP)
Open
Cancel

Adjusting Modem Properties.

Before we can use the script for automatic dial-up, however, we need to make an adjustment to the 'Modem Properties' as follows:

1. Right-Click on the ISP connection profile that you created in Dial-Up Networking Configuration and then click on Properties. This will bring up the General properties of this connection profile:
2. Click on Configure to bring up the modem properties window and select the Options tag.
3. De-select the Bring up terminal window after dialling option and click Ok.
4. Click on Ok again in the general properties window.

Now if you double-click on your ISP connection profile icon or listing item, the connection process to your ISP should be automated. If you have problems, then you may need to contact your ISP to check the scripting details.

Choosing an ISP

In India at most of the places you do not have a choice as far as choosing of an ISP goes. This means that you have the ISP which is given to you as per the area where you are living. However, in case you are blessed to live in a place where there are more than one suppliers, then the following points should be kept in mind while selecting the ISP.

Perhaps the two most important considerations are: the ability of an ISP to provide a free line on-demand and the speed at which the connection operates once established.

The first consideration is determined by the ratio by available lines into the ISP divided by the number of potential users. When you attempts to dial into an ISP for an Internet connection, you are likely to be competing with other users, especially at busy times of the day.

The chances of you getting a free line will be determined by the lines/user ratio. Many ISPs will tell you what this ration is. A low ration (e.g., 5:1) will mean that you will obtain a line almost every time or a higher ratio may mean that you may get a 'number unobtainable' tone on occasion and will need to redial in order to establish a connection.

The speed at which the line operates once connected is not always simply a mater of the speed of your modem. At peak times or whenever there is a heavy demand, the data rate available to each connected user is regulated, thereby apparently slowing down your connection.

The need to do this will in part be determined by the 'trunk' data rate available to the ISP (i.e., the kind of telecommunication connection that the ISP has to the rest of the Internet). Thus the ISPs with the larger trunk connections will be able to provide the maximum data speeds to their users more of the time.

Internet Access Providers – Newsgroups

Most ISPs will also the able to supply access to Newsgroups. As some of the many different areas covered by the thousands of available Newsgroups may be considered of an 'undesirable' nature, some ISPs will block access to these, whilst others allow unlimited access to all available newsgroups.

Newsgroups are made available to the user via a 'Newsgroup Server' at the ISP.

Additional Services of ISPs

Competition between different Internet Access Providers for your Internet account is currently very strong, with new ISPs springing up almost on a daily basis. This means that many are offering additional services in order to tempt you in their particular direction.

Some examples of the additional services an ISP may offer are as follows:

- Free Web Space – hard disk space on the ISPs Web Server to host your own web site. For a typical small business site, more than 1Mb is rarely necessary, unless you plan to provide highly detailed product support information or possibly 'E-Commerce' facilities.
- Web Site Statistics – the ability to supply various types of web site statistics (e.g., to show how many user 'hits' your web site has generated).
- Domain Name Registration Services – registering a unique Domain Name for your organisation's web site. This will reduce a potentially complex web site address (e.g., www.ispsite.co.uk/wwwserver companyname/welcome.htm) to one that your customers will remember more easily (e.g., www.mycompany.com).
- E-mail Forwarding – this would usually be used in conjunction with a unique Domain Name and allows e-mail sent to a web site address to be redirected or 'forwarded' to a specified e-mail account. For example, e-mail sent from a web page link to support@www.company.com' could be forwarded to 'jbloggs@www.company.com', a member of the technical support team.
- CGI Scripting – the 'Common Gateway Interface' language is a means of allowing information to be collected from a web site user and then performing some operation using this information. An example might be a form on your web site that invites potential customers to request information leaflets through the post by inputting their contact details.

This information is then sent to the ISP Web Server, where the CGI Scripting program compiles the details into an e-mail and sends it to you, as well as returning a dynamic web page to the user's browser, informing them that the operation has been successfully completed.

As designing and implementing CGI scripts requires skilled Internet programmers and access to the core functions of an ISP's Internet server, this kind of facility is usually provided as a set of predefined CGI scripts that perform specific functions. However some ISPs aimed at supplying professional services to the web developer, allow custom made CGI scripts to be loaded into a restricted area on the SIP's server.

- Fax/E-mail Services – the ability to convert e-mail into a fax transmission. This can save considerably on international fax transmission costs by providing the same capability at the cost of a local call.
- E-Commerce Services – the ability to securely handle cash transactions over the Internet. This would certainly be useful to those wishing to use the Internet to take direct credit card payments for products ordered from a web site.

Content Providers

Internet access is also now frequently available through what would otherwise be suppliers of information services.

Before the Internet became so widely available, several companies set up publicly available computerised information services. By subscribing to these services, users are able to access a wide range of predefined information services form their PC via a modem connection and using a company specific 'browser' package.

Since the advent of the Internet, these companies now often supply the basic Internet services such as e-mail and web browsing alongside their own 'content' services.

Costs for these services tend to be higher than for a straight forward Internet access account and in some cases the development of the proprietary 'browser' tends to lag behind in the race to implement the latest browser 'standards'.

You can in fact connect your computer to the Internet with the help o a Wizard provided by Window 98 and is called Internet Connection Wizard. It is discussed below.

Using Internet Connection Wizard

This wizard can be accessed through Start/Accessories/Communications/Internet Connection Wizard. This has in all 10 screens, which come on screen one by one and ask you for information to be provided by you.

Once done you will have the internet connection. They are self-explanatory, so no explanation is required. The screens are shown on the next pages.

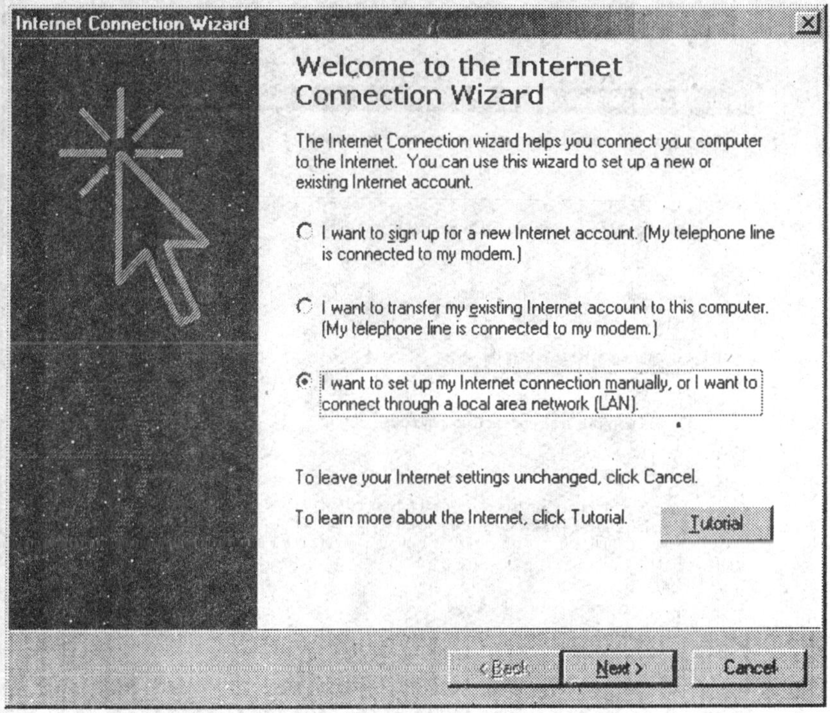

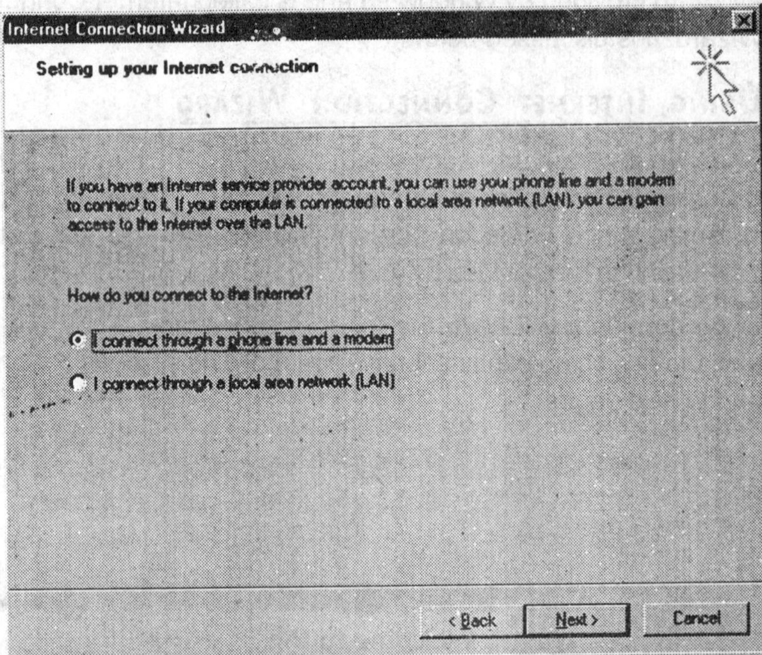
Internet Connection Wizard
Setting up your Internet connection
If you have an Internet service provider account, you can use your phone line and a modem to connect to it. If your computer is connected to a local area network (LAN), you can gain access to the Internet over the LAN.
How do you connect to the Internet?
I connect through a phone line and a modem
I connect through a local area network (LAN)
< Back
Next >
Cancel

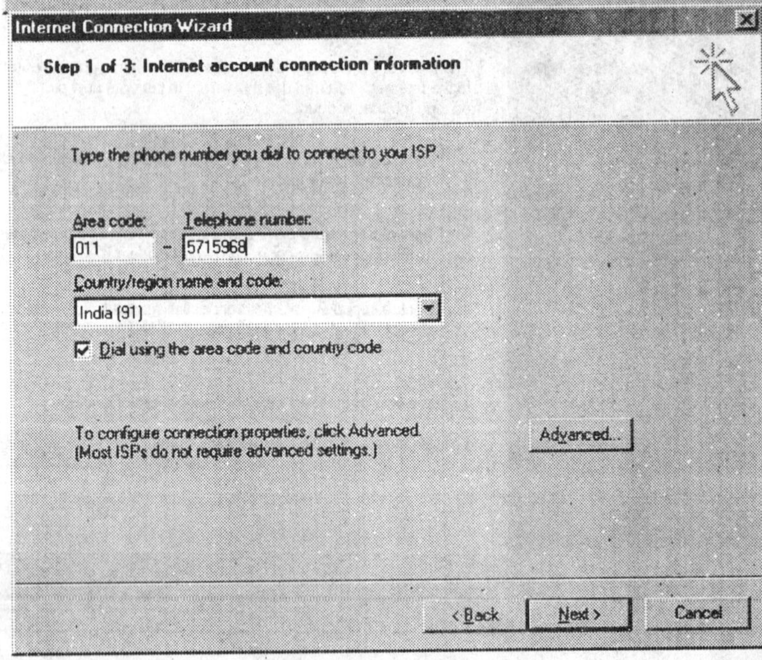
Internet Connection Wizard
Step 1 of 3: Internet account connection information
Type the phone number you dial to connect to your ISP.
Area code:
Telephone number:
011
5715968
Country/region name and code:
India (91)
Dial using the area code and country code
To configure connection properties, click Advanced.
(Most ISPs do not require advanced settings.)
Advanced...
< Back
Next >
Cancel

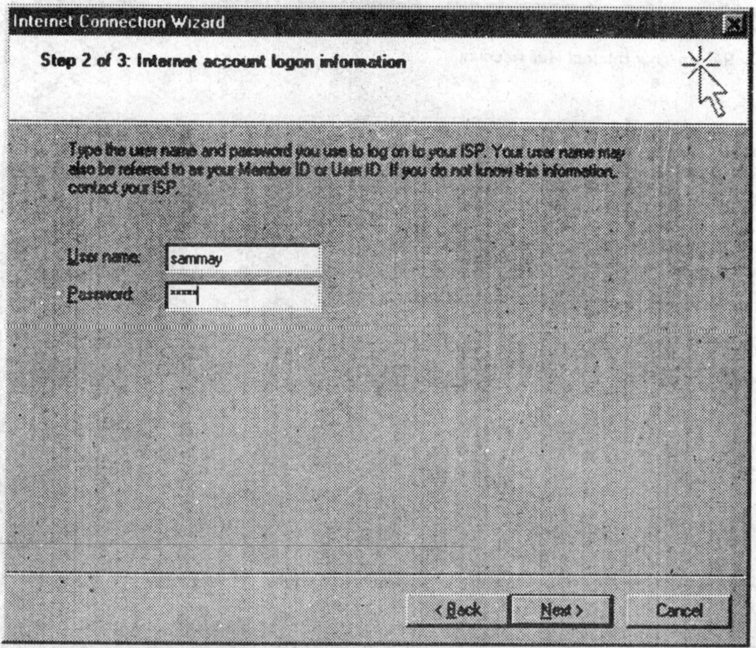
Internet Connection Wizard
Step 2 of 3: Internet account logon information
Type the user name and password you use to log on to your ISP. Your user name may also be referred to as your Member ID or User ID. If you do not know this information, contact your ISP.
User name:
sammay
Password:
< Back
Next >
Cancel

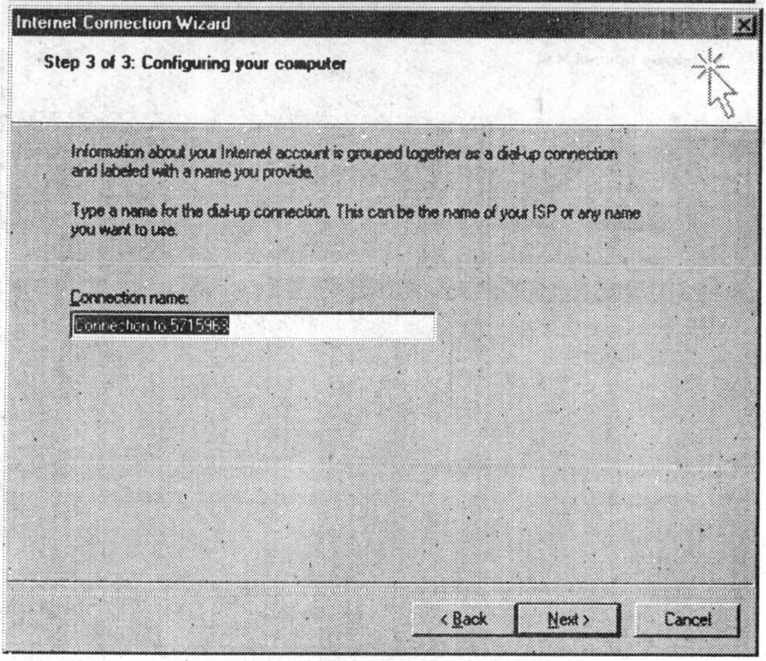
Internet Connection Wizard
Step 3 of 3: Configuring your computer
Information about your Internet account is grouped together as a dial-up connection and labeled with a name you provide.
Type a name for the dial-up connection. This can be the name of your ISP or any name you want to use.
Connection name:
Connection to 5715968
< Back
Next >
Cancel

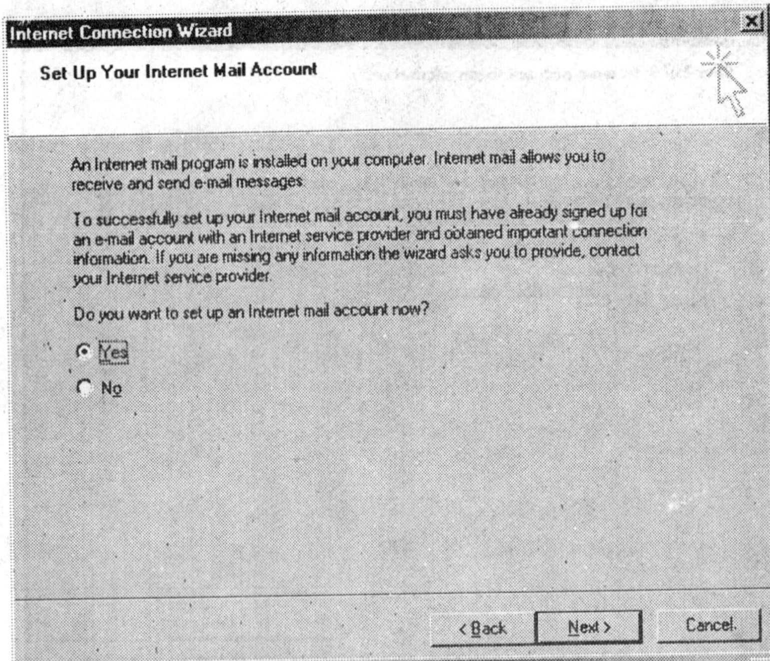
Internet Connection Wizard
Set Up Your Internet Mail Account
An Internet mail program is installed on your computer. Internet mail allows you to receive and send e-mail messages.
To successfully set up your Internet mail account, you must have already signed up for an e-mail account with an Internet service provider and obtained important connection information. If you are missing any information the wizard asks you to provide, contact your Internet service provider.
Do you want to set up an Internet mail account now?
Yes
No
< Back
Next >
Cancel

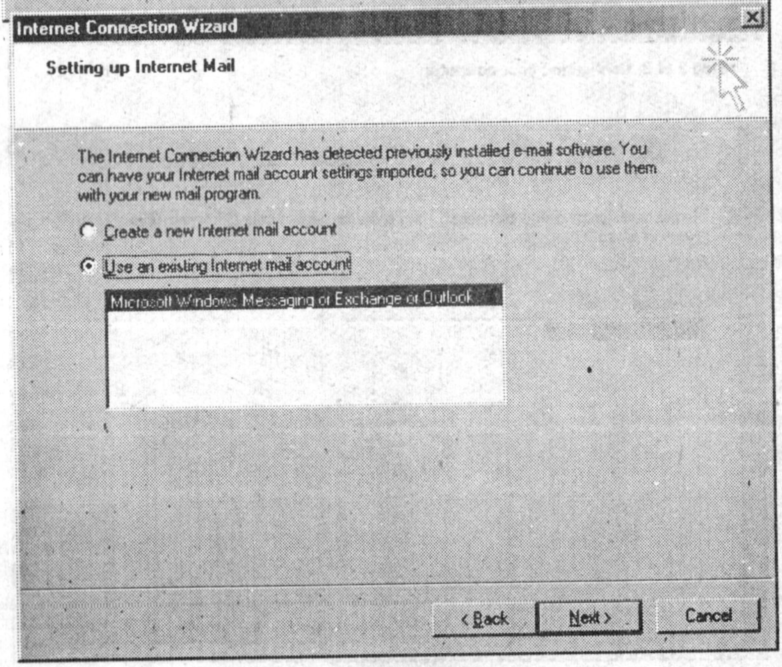
Internet Connection Wizard
Setting up Internet Mail
The Internet Connection Wizard has detected previously installed e-mail software. You can have your Internet mail account settings imported, so you can continue to use them with your new mail program.
Create a new Internet mail account
Use an existing Internet mail account
Microsoft Windows Messaging or Exchange or Outlook
< Back
Next >
Cancel

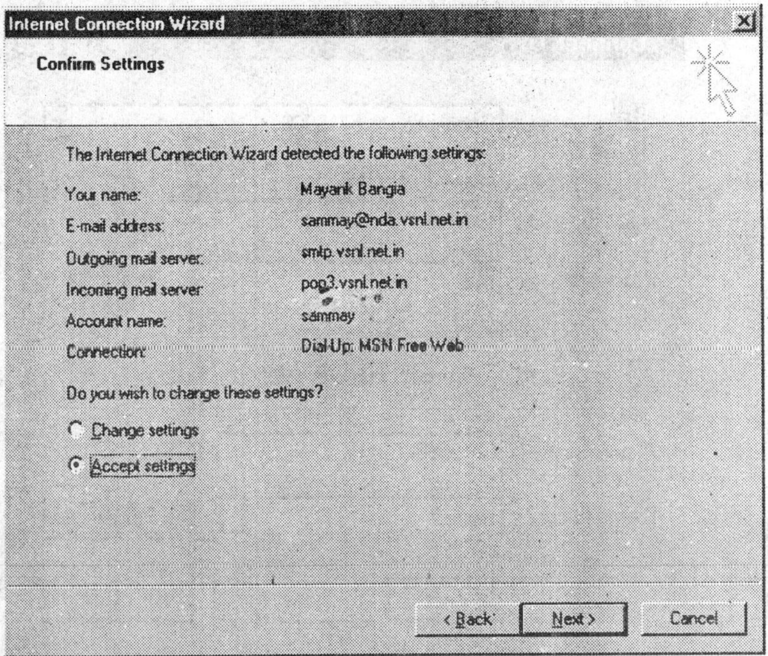
Internet Connection Wizard
Confirm Settings
The Internet Connection Wizard detected the following settings:
Your name: Mayank Bangia
E-mail address: sammay@nda.vsnl.net.in
Outgoing mail server: smtp.vsnl.net.in
Incoming mail server: pop3.vsnl.net.in
Account name: sammay
Connection: Dial-Up: MSN Free Web
Do you wish to change these settings?
Change settings
Accept settings
< Back
Next >
Cancel

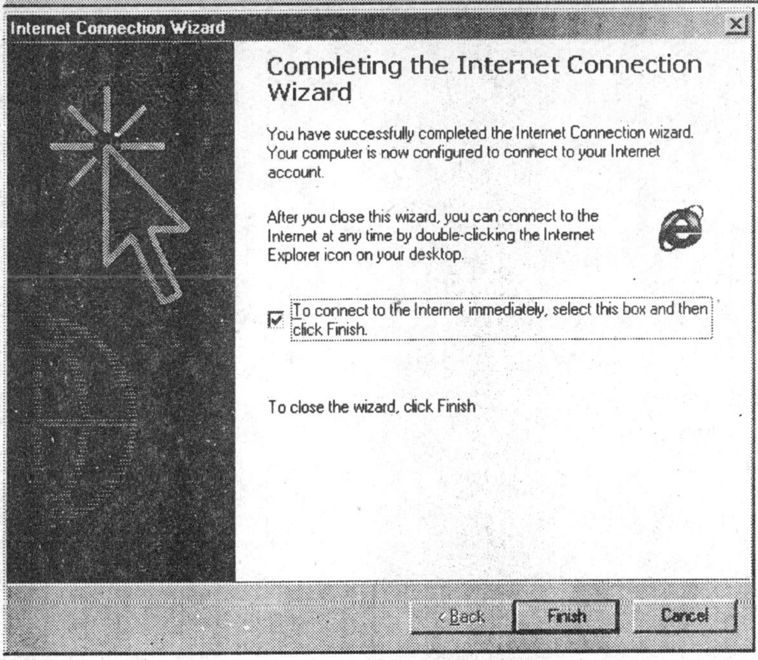
Internet Connection Wizard
Completing the Internet Connection Wizard
You have successfully completed the Internet Connection wizard. Your computer is now configured to connect to your Internet account.
After you close this wizard, you can connect to the Internet at any time by double-clicking the Internet Explorer icon on your desktop.
To connect to the Internet immediately, select this box and then click Finish.
To close the wizard, click Finish
< Back
Finish
Cancel

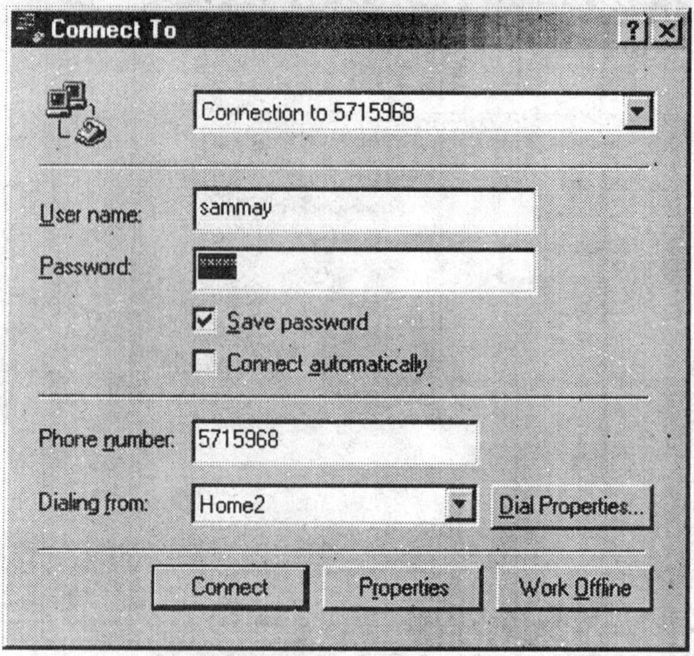
Connect To
Connection to 5715968
User name:
sammay
Password:
Save password
Connect automatically
Phone number:
5715968
Dialing from:
Home2
Dial Properties...
Connect
Properties
Work Offline

7

Networking Software

Introduction

Although it's true that there are many different network products in the marketplace, it's also true that Microsoft has, since the early 1990's done a stellar job ensuring that networking was available to most users of its Windows software.

Although it's true that early versions of Windows for Workgroups were neither terribly fast nor terribly reliable, the networking built into the Windows shell – and later Windows 95, 98, Me and Windows NT operating systems – is both fast and reliable. It's also absurdly easy to configure.

But before I tell you about Windows, I would like to introduce a popular networking solution by the name of Novell Netware. It is no doubt that it ruled the networking solutions for quite some time.

Netware is a sort of personal computer networking standard. Almost every operating system can hook up with Netware in one way or another. Netware can interoperate with everything from old single-tasking DOS to some of the most sophisticated versions of Unix available.

Advantages of NetWare Network

NetWare has some significant advantages. Although NetWare can be a bear to install, configure and tune, it has some great features:

Speed and Scalability

The core of NetWare is surprisingly efficient. It keeps in memory a record of files stored on it; as a result, it can access and serves files to users blazingly fast. For a small network, the speed with which a server can deliver files to users isn't critical because the server is usually not highly stressed. However, NetWare continues to deliver great performance as the number of client users increases.

The trade press continues to test NetWare and Internetware products; in a significant percentage of the tests, NetWare is the fastest PC-based file and print server. It also has tremendous scalability; one NetWare server can handle far more clients than almost any other PC-based NOS.

Long Filenames

In response to OS/2 Windows 95, Windows 2000 and Macintosh computers, NetWare also has support for long filenames. To use long filenames, however, special software (called OS2.NAM, LONG.NAM or MAC.NAM) must be loaded to support the name space or the special area on the disk that stores long filenames.

Long-filename support must be loaded before the operating system begins to access NetWare partitions with long-filename support, but once it's loaded, NetWare can support filenames upto 31 characters. This is more significant than it sounds. Even though some operating systems can save 255-characters filenames, 31 characters are sufficient to name most files both descriptively and uniquely.

Built-in Hierarchical Organization

NetWare 5.x comes with a built-in system for building, organizing and managing hierarchical networks. This system, called NetWare Directory Services (NDS), is capable of handling the network-organizational needs of a global organization as well as the single server local network.

NDS is Novell's method for organizing all the elements of an enterprise network. In an NDS network, a single logon provides access to the same resources, no matter where on the network the user logs on. NDS is relatively complex; if you have to build a network across multiple sites, later versions and NDS provide a powerful enabling tool. Novell's per-server scalability is the stuff of legend, but even a single sever has limits.

When Novell designed NetWare 4.x, the company realized that the flat-file single-server log on limit that NetWare 3.x effectively imposed needed revision.

The result of Novell's effort was NDS. In NDS, everything – every user, every computer, every printer, every server, every site – is an object that can be managed. It's great solution and is what is sustaining Novell in the market versus Unix and Windows 2000 Server's encroachment on its territory.

As a matter of fact, Novell has released NDS software for Unix, IBM's OS/390 mainframe operating system and every flavor of Windows. Of course, with the release of Windows 2000, Microsoft has its Active Directory, which duplicates many of NDS' functions.

Reliability

NetWare has been in existence since the early 1980s. As a result, Novell has largely worked out the bugs within the operating system. Even NetWare 4.x, a total rewrite of NetWare introduced in the mid-1990s, was remarkably stable in its first release. Subsequent releases have brought even more stability to this NOS.

It is not uncommon to see properly configured NetWare servers that have been running for months (or, in some cases, years) without a reboot. NetWare has a high tolerance for errors and can often manage a problem without ABENDing or crashing.

Among all the major NOS manufacturers, Novell stands alone in its approach to updating its server software. The company periodically releases complete software patches to fix recently discovered bugs and it's possible in many cases to load only the patch modules that your server requires instead of loading a whole set of patches.

Only Unix used to offer this functionality and while Microsoft does make some individual patches available, they generally recommend loading a service pack or collection of patches, en masse. Novell's Web site, www.novell.com, enables the user to research and download software quite easily – and there's wealth of information available there, as well.

Disadvantages of a NetWare Network

In some ways, Novell has unfortunately been a victim of its own success. In its push to become the one perfect enterprise Intel-computer network operating system – which, in many ways, it is – the company concentrated on its core strengths (file and print services) at the expense of its application services and ease of administration.

Expensive to Administer

As NetWare eclipsed all other PC-based Network Operating Systems, Novell focused on the large-corporate marketplace to the detriment of its smaller customers, denying those customers reasonably priced direct access to Novell's technical support system.

Since 1989, instead of going directly to Novell with a problem, customers, no matter how small, have had to engage the services of a Certified NetWare Engineer (CNE). CNEs are professionals trained in NetWare configuration, design and troubleshooting. CNE service is relatively expensive; it's not uncommon to see $150 hourly charges for it.

Weak Application Services

NetWare was designed to function primarily as a file and print server. However, since NetWare was designed, the requirements for servers have expanded tremendously. In the early days of networking, sharing files and printer was sufficient. With the increased power of personal computers, however, servers have begun to run applications formerly performed on mainframes or minicomputers.

Such services include database management and network management. Although Novell has made a valiant effort to break into the application server market, it currently plays a distant third to Unix and Windows 2000.

Novell's NetWare Application Launcher is making inroads as a software distribution system and has revitalized use of NetWare on some networks.

Difficult to Administer

Last and probably most problematic for neophyte networkers, NetWare is relatively difficult to administer. Unlike Windows 2000, NetWare doesn't have a graphical interface at the server console. Although a graphical interface isn't absolutely necessary, it does make administrative tasks easier to accomplish.

Novell has addressed this fault by writing Netadmin and NWAdmin, two graphical NetWare management utilities that run under DOS and Windows, respectively. These utilities go a long way toward easing the pain of administering NetWare servers, but they still don't run at the server console itself.

Windows Operating Systems

When Microsoft introduced Windows for Workgroups in the early 1990s, it knew that the product had to satisfy two markets to succeed. The first was the corporate market, which had found that Windows 3.x left a great deal to be desired in terms of its capability to function in a network setting.

The second was the emerging small-network market, the small offices, libraries and yes, even the home networks of computer users eager to share files and printers. To say that Microsoft succeeded beyond its wildest dreams would be incorrect. Although the company sold a lot of copies of Windows for Workgroups, it also took some well-deserved flak for the shortcomings of the product.

People complained that it didn't like the fact that running more than one protocol on Windows for Workgroups was a recipe for disaster the system expanded so much memory in the process of networking that there wasn't much memory left for applications. Not everyone, however, was upset by the shortcomings of Windows for Workgroups. The only protocol included with Windows for Workgroups was NetBEUI, so third-party vendors were able to sell various other protocols (mostly NetWare IPX and TCP/IP) to users for whom NetBEUI's single-segment-networking wasn't a viable option.

Although this represented an additional expense for large corporate networkers whose networks relied on TCP/IP, in the long run, the arrangement turned out to be good for PC buyers. During this period, firms such as FTP Software, Hummingbrid and others entered the PC software market in earnest. Their entry into the market revealed a shift in the attitude of corporate networking toward personal computers:

Because they could run TCP/IP and connect to already-existing corporate resources, they were to be treated as acceptable. Although Windows for Workgroups had its shortcomings, it set a precedent: All future Microsoft operating system products would be networkable. In a world of poorly connected PC operating systems, this was both a revelation and a revolution.

Windows 95, 98 and Me

Windows for Wokgroups was superseded in later 1995 by Windows 95, Microsoft's first attempt at a 32-bit consumer operating system. Windows 95's networking components were a great deal more comprehensive than those of Windows for Workgroups. Windows 95 included NetBEUI, that flat namespace, nonroutable protocol that Micorsoft used for very small networks, an IPOX-compatible protocol for use with Novell Netware networks and a surprisingly capable IP stack. Because networking consumers had expressed a desire to simplify dial-up networking, Microsoft included a capable (and relatively simple-to-configure) dial-up networking client.

Windows 95, intended to be all things to most people, rapidly found broad acceptance among PC manufacturers who sold it on desktop compute systems. In 1998, Microsoft released a new operating system called Windows 98 that built on the capabilities of Windows 95.

Given Microsoft's sudden and intense focuses on Internet capable products, it had a desktop that was intimately tried to Internet tied to Internet and other TCP/IP resources and new software like Peer Web Server, which enabled anyone with Windows 98 on their PC to host Web pages.

It also had better power management and better overall stability than Windows 95 and it consequently sold like hotcakes. The latest iteration in this family is Windows Me. Released in September 2000, it is related to Windows 98 as 98 was to 95 – an update with some new features, better networking, some minor changes.

Windows NT Workstation and Windows 2000 Professional

In 1993, between the launch of Windows for Workgroups and Windows 95, Microsoft released its enterprise 32-bit operating system, Windows NT, with surprisingly little fanfare. It's understandable; Windows NT 3.1 the initial version of Microsoft's enterprise level operating system, was not as capable as users would have liked.

It was big and slow and it did not run 16-bit applications (which made up the vast bulk of the Windows software market at that time) particularly well. Worst of all, it did not network well at all – there was very little software to allow it to tie into other computers.

About a year and a half after the release of Windows NT 3.1, however, Microsoft release Windows NT 3.5 NT 3.5 was not simply a minor upgrade; it was a fundamental rewrite of NT with a variety of options added that made it network friendly right out of the box.

Microsoft had also, in the interim, firmed up its networking strategy, in the process dividing NT into two operating systems: Windows NT server, which was capable of managing domains or logical of computers, in much the same fashion as a NetWare or Unix server; and Windows NT workstation, which had no less connectivity than its server-oriented sibling but had the additional opportunity to participate in workgroups, Micorsoft's term for peer resource sharing.

Windows NT workstation continued to evolve to version 4.0, which shares a common interface with Windows 95 and 98. Windows NT Workstation 4.0 could connect to a variety of networks, as can its other Windows siblings and it offers much greater stability because each application (including a great deal of the networking software) runs in separate memory spaces – which (ideally) ensures that no application can grab memory that other applications (or the operating system) are using.

The latest iteration in this branch of Microsoft's family tree is Windows 2000 Professional. Windows 2000 Professional is a desktop operating system that Microsoft markets to businesses rather than home users. Its appearance is closer to Windows 98 than Windows NT 4.0 and the networking configuration tools have changed quite radically for the better – it's much easier to configure now.

In additional, it's also possible to make a lot of network changes without rebooting the system, a practice for which Windows NT was notorious. In a workgroup (that is, a Windows network without a Windows NT or 2000 Server managing the whole network) configuration, any number of this family of operating systems can connect to each other, assuming that the correct parameters are in place. The next section acquaints you with Windows workgroup networking concepts.

About Windows 2000 Server

When Microsoft released Windows NT version 3.5, they elected to separate Windows NT Workstation 3.5 from the NT Advanced Serve product and marketed them separately as Windows NT Workstation and Windows 2000 Server. Over time, Windows NT Workstation has evolved into Windows 2000 Professional, targeted at the desktop and Windows 2000 Server has evolved into Windows 2000 Advanced Server.

Windows 2000 Professional is fundamentally intended for use on the desktop of a workstation computer. Windows 2000 Advanced Server, by contrast, is packaged with many utilities that enable it to administer and manage a network much better than Windows 2000 Professional.

Windows 2000 Server is by all accounts a robust, easy-to-manage operating system. Its graphical user interface is similar to Windows 98 and Me, which eases the learning curve. The similarity of the interface to Microsoft's other offerings makes installation and most configuration tasks relatively simple. At this point, Windows 2000 is a relatively mature product.

It's got a new name and a modified interface, but it's still built on the Windows NT code that Microsoft has been working on since 1993. It's still got some shortcomings (it doesn't scale as well as Unix, it lacks a real-time disk defragmenter, it's still got some shortcomings (it doesn't scale as well as Unix, it lacks a real-time disk defragmenter, it's got a few security issues and so on) but all in all, it's reasonable server operating system.

Microsoft has a long history of aggressively tackling tough markets and beating the competition and there's little doubt that they'll continue to take this tack with Windows 2000 Server. Windows 2000 Server can use the same variety of network protocols as Windows 2000 Professional.

The main difference between 2000 Professional and 2000 Server's networking capabilities is that the latter doesn't use the workgroup configurations. Instead, it groups computers using an organizational scheme Microsoft calls domains.

Windows 2000 Server's File Systems

Microsoft built its Windows NT and Windows NT-derived products, such as Windows 2000 Professional, from a clean sheet. As a result, NT has a wide variety of options, including options for two file systems.

Windows NT can use one or both of two local file systems (ways of organizing the local hard drives), which offers a great deal of flexibility. B^cause selecting the file system you want to use is part of the installation routine, you should know what these file systems are:

File Allocation Table (FAT)

FAT is a legacy from MS-DOS and Windows 95. It supports filenames that must follow a strict pattern of eight characters or less, followed by a period, followed by a three-letter extension (such as RADME.TXT).

This has changed somewhat, as has the file system in Windows 2000; if you use a FAT file system, it's called FAT32 and it supports long filenames, although it lacks the security of NTFS.

NT File System (NFTS)

In an attempt to gain the advantages of IBM's OS/2 High Performance File System (HPFS) with additional capabilities, Microsoft designed its own file system for NT/200 and called it (naturally) NT File System.

NTFS allows long filenames (up to 254 characters) and can work with Windows 95, OS/2

Windows 2000 Server Networking Basics

Microsoft Windows 2000 (and in fact, all Microsoft networking products) communicates using Server Message Block (SMB), a protocol for requesting remote resources. SMB is part of the structure that underlines NetBIOS Extended User Interface (NetBEUI), NetBIOS's younger, far more capable sibling.

NetBEUI also includes NetBIOS Frames (NBF), the protocol that handles the OSI layer 4 tasks (the TCP in TCP/IP), SMB is pretty much the "core" protocol of Windows 2000 Server in the same way that NetWare Core Protocol (NCP) is the core of NetWare – you don't see a lot about either protocol (most of the attention is paid to protocols such as IPX, NetBEUI and TCP/IP instead), but they're there.

Unix as a Network Operating System

Selecting Unix for local network – or even a first network – is not necessarily a bad choice. The software with which it is possible to build a small local network is relatively low cost (Linux is available as a free download on the Web or on CD-ROM for about S30; FreeBSD, a version of BSD Unix that's free of copyright restrictions, is also available for $30 or so on CD-ROM) and provides a fine introduction to Unix and Unix-style systems.

Although Unix is not user-hostile, neither is it simple; you'll need a book specifically dedicated to Unix, Linux or FreeBSD to get the server running.

If you use it, you'll learn a great deal and wind up with a system that is fast, reliable and (typically) less prone to user-created problems than almost any of the other operating systems described in this chapter.

Unix makes a great network operating system. It's got great file services via nfs, it's the best Webserver in the world (the freeware Apache Webserver running on Linux is used by more Webwerver than any other Webserver software in the world), the sendmail email program is the world standard for exchanging email between servers and there are a host of other services that Unix can provide. It's worth the learning curve.

Things That Go Together: Networking and Unix

In the late 1980s and early 1990s, networking burst open and all of a sudden, anyone who could network, did. Ethernet, long a mainstay of Unix businesses environments, was suddenly everywhere – and when it showed up, everyone wanted to be able to run TCP/IP and network with existing Unix systems.

Users wanted to be able to access their terminal applications over the network because it was faster and more reliable. To accomplish this, a new class of software appeared on PCs: terminal emulator software. Terminal emulators offered people with PCs the capability to connect to Unix systems using Ethernet networking. It worked, but it wasn't good enough; it was slow and it offered only a limited range of features. Over time, vendors became aware that servers in the PC would were doing more than simply running specific applications for users.

Servers were acting as file repositories, print servers, communications servers and the like. PC users wanted to have the same type of client/server connections to Unix systems that they had with their NetWare servers. But initially, there was no way to mount a Unix drive on a PC system – that is, there was no way that a PC could see a Unix system as another network drive letter.

Remote File Systems: nfs

Files don't exist in a vacuum on a network. They need to be shared to be useful. Sun Microsystems realized that the marketplace needed a way to allow PC users to see Unix server hard drives as network hard drives. Consequently they ported their Network File System (nfs) software to personal computers.

Nfs has long been a mainstay of the Unix world, since it enables Unix systems to gain access to files on remote systems as if they were stored locally. PC-nfs provided the facility for remote computers to see a Unix disk volume in their own file system – whether the volume was seen as another drive letter (as in Windows) or as another directory in the local file system (as in Unix).

When using nfs, PC simply sees a Unix system's hard drive as another network drive. nfs offered a great way to share Unix file resources with personal computes. PC-nfs was a smash hit from the beginning. It enabled Unix systems to work with a variety of other computers as though the Unix system was local. It could work in the local network or across the wide area link – it solved a lot of problems.

Currently, the market has expanded and there are a number of vendors (Hummingbird, WRQ and others) who offer nfs connectivity in their Unix host connectivity packages. Even Microsoft has gotten into the act with their Unix Services for Windows NT package.

Other Remote File Systems: afs, dfs and Samba

Sometimes, however, nfs didn't serve all the needs of users quite right. Two responses to nfs were Andrew File System (afs) and distributed file system (dfs). Both offered a slightly different range of features than nfs. To get into the differences, however, would be delving into esorterica.

Windows machines, however, were still outside the range of most remove file systems, except for PC-nfs. To remedy this situation, a new product called Samba was written in the early 1990s. Samba is a Unix implementation of Microsoft's Server Message Block protocol (SMB, hence "samba").

Samba enables Unix to share its resources just as if they were shared from a Windows machine. It's easy to use; like a great deal of Unix software, it's available at no charge from a variety of sites on the Internet and has already been compiled for a huge number of different Unix versions. In fact, using Samba, Linux systems can function as Windows NT domain servers (although they don't yet work with Windows 2000's Active Directory).

Basic Windows Networking Concepts

Basic Windows networking is quite simple. There are three simple concepts to understand that go a long way toward explaining Microsoft networking: sharing, arbitrary sharing and workgroups. There are some other concepts that you'll need to learn about such as Windows 2000 Server domains and Active Directory. This is about networking with Windows at the desktop level.

Sharing

The first major concept in Microsoft networking is sharing. When you were a kid, you probably had some object that others converted ... and that you jealously clutched, fearful of losing. Adults, who understood the social milieu better than your childhood self, probably suggested that you allow another child to use your object to desire, saying, "share be nice."

A lot of the time, you tried to put conditions on the use of the shared object, conditions that were usually completely disregarded or complained about until you were convinced to remove the restriction.

With Windows networking, you're in the same position again. Your drive space and printers are your precious objects; in Windows peer networking, you share them so that other users can access them. But this is where it gets better being a kid: You get to set conditions for use, such as which users the allowed to access resources and when they are allowed to use them and other users have to go along with it.

Sharing represents a huge simplification of resource sharing. It's useful way to ensure that other users on a network can have access to a given workstation's file and print resources. Its only downside is that when an NT Server isn't involved, it's arbitrary and high maintenance.

Consequently, the printer and file-sharing described here is not for use in large enterprise networks; this is how resources are shared in a smaller group of computers that may or may not have a server.

Arbitrary Sharing

The second of the three concepts is that sharing is arbitrary. If you a whole drive or a folder on your local drive any authorized user can connect to it and assign it a drive letter (for example, h:\) on his or her workstation. Likewise with printers: If you share a printer, any other user with access rights can connect to it and print to it.

However, each workstation that has access to your file and print resources has to decide to connect to them. Then they get confused because the resources on one machine aren't in the same locations as the resources on the computer the user normally uses.

This calls up another shortcoming of Microsoft networking: inconsistent naming of resources on remote systems. It's something that Microsoft would do well to change, in the author's opinions.

Workgroups

The third concept of Windows peer networking is workgroups. Windows for Workgroups was not named arbitrarily; it was named after the atomic unit of network organization in Microsoft's initial take of the networking world. In Windows terms, a workgroup is a group of computers that share a common workgroup name.

Workgroups don't enforce security or provide any particular resource other than making the network easier for users to browse – it doesn't provide any particular networking function other than user-level organization. More than one workgroup can exist on a given physical network; in fact, an almost unlimited number of workgroups can exist.

Every computer can have its own workgroup – though the utility of doing so is questionable. If your network will be divided between a sales staff and a technical staff, you might divide your network into two workgroups.

One, called SALES, connects your sales staff together; the other, called TECH, ties your technical users together. If a user from either group needs a resource on a machine in the other workgroup, that user can connect to it, but most of the time he or she is working within his or her own workgroup. This kind of networking provides a user-level logical segmentation of the networks and can help make resources easier for users to find.

Microsoft BackOffice

Microsoft has created an all-in-one server package called BackOffice that provides most of the admistrative functions a network requires.

It consists of the following:

Exchange Server

A groupware and messaging server that can handle Internet-compliant email.

SQL Server

A database management system that is quite robust.

Systems Management Server (SMS)

A network management package that enables administrators to install software and provide remote technical support to users.

Systems Network Architecture Server (SNA Server)

This enables Windows 2000 to connect to IBM midrange and mainframe computers.

Internet Information Server (IIS)

This turns an NT server into an Internet server for the World Wide Web, FTP, Gopher, and other services.

8

Glossary of Networking

10BASE-2

Ethernet networking running on coaxial cable. Also called thinnet or cheapernet, 10BASE-2 supports network segments up to 185 meters in length. It is a bus topology and cannot withstand any interruption in any cable between two computers.

10BASE-5

Also called yellow-cable Ethernet, 10BASE-5 is similar to 10BASE-2 but uses a thicker cable. Each computer attached to a 10BASE-5 segment has a device called a transceiver tat connects the computer to the network wire. 10BASE-5 is a bus topology and cannot withstand disconnections of any computers.

10BASE-T

Ethernet in a star topology. 10BASE-T uses unshielded twisted-pair wiring(UTP) with eight connectors terminated according to specific standards called TIAA 568B. Because it is a star topology. 10BASE-T is much more robust than 10BASE-2 or 10BASE-5.

56K

A digital phone line that can carry data at speeds of up to 56 kilobits per second.

adapter card

This definition applies primarily to Intel-compatible computers. An adapter card is an electronic assembly that connects to a computer through a standard interface (see card-slot interface, later in this glossary) called a card slot. Adapter cards can provide a variety of services to the computer, including vide, network, modem and other function as required.

Administration

An impossible task that involves figuring out how to keep a network running without problems all the time. Part V of this book, "Introduction to Network Administration," is dedicated to this topic.

analog

Based on waveforms rather than on binary patterns of voltage.

analog phone line

A phone line that transmits the sound of your voice as a waveform (like a radio wave). Analog phone lines are common; chances are that analog phone lines are what you have your home phone plugged into. To transmit data over an analog phone line, you must convert it from digital data to sound – that's why modems (devices that convert data to sound) make funny-sounding squawks and hisses. That's digital data being converted to sound.

application

A software program intended to accomplish a single task. For example, Microsoft Word is intended to ease document preparation.

ARPA

Advanced Research Projects Agency, the government group responsible for starting the Internet.

ASCII

American Standard Code for Information Interchange, a way that computers for mat 1s and 0s (binary code, which computers can understand) into the alphabet, numerals and other characters that human can understand

ATM

Asynchronous Transfer Mode, a new topology for transmitting data across a network. TM is complex but has many advantages compared to older topologies such as Ethernet and Token Ring. AT offers Quality of Service and a standard frame (or "cell") size. ATM is rarely used on small networks because of its cost; it is most commonly used in large WAN networks.

authentication

The process of ensuring, as much as possible, that logons and messages from a user (such as a password or email) originate from an authorised source.

backbone

A series of very high-speed phone lines (ranging from 155 to 622) megabits per second – really fast!) that phone companies use to transmit high volumes of traffic. Compare this speed to that of your LAN, where data moves at 10 megabits per second and you begin to see why it's called the backbone. New technologies are offering increased speed of over a gigabit per second, which will be useful as more people want to sue the Internet.

backward compatibility

The capability of a software or hardware product to work with earlier versions of itself.

bandwidth

The measurement of the amount of data a particular medium can carry. For example, the bandwidth of the average phone line is only about 33.6 kilobits per second; the bandwidth for a TI digital phone line is 1.544 megabits per second.

batch processing

A situation common in early mainframe environments in which many tasks were scheduled to run at a specific time late in the evening. The user never directly interacted with the computer in batch processing.

binary

Having only two states; used to describe the base 2 arithmetic that computers use. In binary notation, 1,2,3,4,5 is represented as 1, 10, 11, 100, 101. The place value of each place in binary notation doubles with each digits to the left of the decimal point, hence 16, 8, 4, 2, 1. Contrast this with decimal notation base 10), in which each place value is equal to ten times that of the column to its right.

bit

Once piece of information, represented as a 1 or a 0. To the computer, a bit is actually a difference in voltage: high voltage represents a 1, how voltage represents a 0.

bridge

A device that links different networks together so that they form a single logical network. Bridges work at layer 2 of the OSI model.

browser

A program that provides a way to view and read the documents available on the World Wide Web. Netscape Navigator and Microsoft Internet Explorer are browsers.

bus topology

A network topology in which all computers are serially connected to a length of cable. Bus networks are not terribly reliable; if one cable segment goes bad, the whole network fails. 10BASE-2 and 10BASE-5 are examples of bus networks.

byte

Eight bits (also called one octet when discussing TCP/IP). A byte is equal to one character; for example, the letter e is one byte. One byte (eight bits) can represent 256 numbers (0 to 255) in binary.

C programming language

Also known as "C", a high-level computer language developed by Brian Kernighan and Dennis Ritchie at Bell Labs. The C language enables programmes to write code that can be compiled to run on different types of computers' C programming is widely regarded as a cross between an art and a science.

cable modem

A device used by cable providers to provide high-speed data access using cable as the media.

card-slot interface

The place in which adapter cards are installed in Intel-compatible personal computers. Card-slot interfaces come in several varieties: ISA, EISA, VESA (now outdated) and PCI.

CDPD

Cellular Digital Packet Data, the most common way to send data over wireless links. Most commonly, CDPD uses the 2.4GHz radio spectrum.

cheapernet

A colloquial name for 10BASE-2, so called because it is just about the least expensive type of network one can build.

checksum

A part of packet header that ensures that the packet has not been damaged during transmission across the network. A checksum is a number calculated on-the-fly based on the size of the packet; if the checksum is incorrect, the receiving computer discards the packet and asks the originating computer to resend it.

ciphertext

The text on an encoded message. Ciphertext is not readable unless it is decrupted into plaintext. In other words, up c fps opu up cf is an example of a ciphertext message.

CIR

Committed Information Rate, a guarantee from the provider of a digital phone line service (usually your local telephone company) that ensures the slowest data transmission speed your network will ever have. CIR is usually calculated at a fraction of the rated line speed; for example a 128K frame relay line often has a CIR of 64K, or 50% of the bandwidth.

client

A computer that uses the resources shared by server computers.

client/server

A network in which the processing is distributed between a server and a client, each with specific roles. Also used to describe networks with dedicated servers. Opposite of peer-to-peer.

clustering

In networking, clustering is aggregating several servers so that if one of them fails, other servers seamlessly take over.

coaxial cable

A two-conductor cable with a solid center conductor and a braided outer conductor. Coaxial cable is used for 10BASE-2 networks and is similar to the cable used for cable TV.

collision

In terms of networking, what happens when two computers attempt to transmit data on the same network wire at the same time. Doing so creates a conflict; both computers sense the collision, stop transmitting and wait a random amount of time before retransmitting.

collision domain

The group of computers that communicate on a single network wire. Each computer in a collision domain listens to every other computer in the collision domain; each computer can transmit data only when no other computer is currently transmitting.

compiler

A program that takes computer source code (which is just plain text, the same kind you see in Windows Notepad or the DOS Edit utility) and translates it into machine language, which is a string of instructions that the computer can execute. Compilers are synonymous with Unix; almost every variety of Unix is packaged with at least a C compiler. Many versions of Unix now also come with C++ compilers. Compilers exist for many languages; C is simply the most common.

concentrator

Also called a hub or MAU, a concentrator helps ensure the robustness of the network by making sure that the network can't be disconnected because of a single cable failure.

configuration management

The art (or science) of ensuring (from a central console) that user workstations have the correct hardware and software installed and that the software and hardware is set up according to consensual and preset standards.

CPU

Central Processing Unit, the microprocessor inside a computer that enables it to function. Examples of CPUs include Intel's Pentium and Pentium Pro, Motorola's PowerPC and Digital Equipment Corporation's Alpha chips.

cracker

Someone who makes unauthorized accesses into other's computer systems, usually maliciously. Not the same as hacker.

CSMA/CD

Carrier Sense Multiple Access/Collision Detection, the means by which computers exchange data in Ethernet networks.

CSU/DSU

Channel Service Unit/Data Service Unit, a device that changes local network packets into packets that can be transmitted over a WAN.

DARPA

Defense Advanced Research Projects Agency, or ARPA after it was taken over by the military.

database

A file or collection of data structured in logical relationships. For example, the phone book is a database on paper, with names in one column and phone numbers in another column.

decimal

The way of writing numbers we sue all the time; base 10. In base 10, you count from 1 to 9 like this: 1, 2, 3, 4, 5, 6, 7, 8, 9. Contrast this with binary and hexadecimal notation.

denial-of-service attack

An attack on Internet-connected computer that forces it to cease performing its designated function (Web serving, file serving, etc).

device driver

Software that controls specific hardware on your computer. For example, the software that controls your mouse and keyboard is a device driver.

DHCP

Dynamic Host Configuration Protocol, a piece of the TCP/IP protocol suite that handles the automatic assignment of IP addresses to clients.

dial-on-demand

Whenever a user needs a resource on another LAN (a file, database access, whatever) the local LAN catches the request and dials the remote LAN using either garden-variety Plain Old Telephone Service (POTS) or a switched digital phone line such as Integrated Services Digital Network (ISDN).

digital

A data transmission type based on data that has been binary encoded (that is, data that has been formatted into 1s and 0s).

digital phone line

A phone line that converts the sound of your voice into digital data.

Digital phone lines work better for computers than analog phone lines because computers transmit information digitally. Digitally phone lines are often used for WANs in which data has to be transmitted at high speeds over long distances.

directory services

A set of tools that enable network administrators to provide users with access to certain specific resources independent of where on the network the uses log in. In other words, if Tom in Marketing has access to server1 and Server2 but no access to Server3, he can access only to Server1 and Server2 regardless of whether he logs into the network on a computer in Marketing, Production or Administration. As networks have grown more complex and required management of greater number of users, directory services have become a saving grace for network administrators trying to manage access across thousand-plus-user, multisite networks.

disk

A device that stores digital 1s and 0s (also called bits) on magnetic media such as a hard drive or floppy drive. CD-ROM drives use light rather than electrical impulses to retrieve data.

DNS

Domain Naming System, the pieces of the TCP/IP protocol suite that resolve IP addresses to names. For example, DNS resolves 192.168.1.5 to alice.library.net.

domain

A group of computers whose logon across the network is authenticated through the NR server. Essentially, a domain takes authentication out of the hands of the individual workstations and centralizes it on the server.

DSL

Digital Subscriber Line, a means by which the phone company provides high-speed digital data services over standard two-pair copper wire.

email

Electronic mail, a way of sending text and files across a network with postal-mail-like notification.

encapsulation

The process of taking a packet of one protocol and putting another protocol's information around it. Equivalent to taking a letter, sealing it in an envelope, addressing that envelope and then placing the first, sealed envelope into a second envelope addressed in a different language. It's not really efficient and it wastes materials and time. Unfortunately, that's often the only way to accomplish something.

encryption key

A series of letters and numbers used to make plaintext messages into ciphertexts. An encryption key's security depends on how long it is.

error correction

The process of ensuring that data transferred across the wire is done so correctly. Typically, error correction work by using a checksum to determine whether or not data has been corrupted in transfer. The process of error correction takes a certain amount of the bandwidth of any connection. The more failure-prone the connection is, the more robust (and hence, the larger in bits) the error correction should be in relation to the entire bandwidth. In other words, a dial-up line tends to be noisy and unreliable, so error correction takes up a lot of the connection's bandwidth. By contrast, a digital connection such as a TI is much cleaner and hence has less error correction.

Ethernet

A local area network (LAN) topology based on a method called Carrier Sense Multiple Access/Collision Detection. Ethernet comes in many varieties – the specification is available in IEEE 802.3. Other versions of Ethernet include 802.2, SNAP and II. Ethernet is, by all accounts, the most common network topology in the world today.

fail over

The logical extension of fault tolerance. In a fail-over system, there are two (or occasionally more) servers, each with identical copies of a master server's drives and resources. If the master server fails, the backup server takes over dynamically and users never see the difference (except for a small and brief slowdown).

fault tolerance or redundancy

The capability of a computer system to shrug off failure of a device and continue operating normally. Generally, fault-tolerant devices send a message to an administrative user when a particular device fails so that the device can be replaced. Fault tolerance is often implemented by simply adding a second device (a second hard drive, network card, or whatever). Of late, however, IBM-compatible computers are beginning to use clustering for fault tolerance; that's when a whole extra machine is on standby, waiting for the first one to fail. See also clustering.

FDDI

Fiber Distributed data Interface, a method of transmitting data across a network using lasers and pulses of light sent over a glass fiber cable rather than sending electricity over a copper wire.

fiber

Optical fiber is used instead of copper wire in some networks. It looks like coaxial cable with flexible strands of glass in the center rather than copper wire.

firewall

A computer that controls access to an Internet-connected network.

frame relay

A method of reframing (or repacketizing) already-packetized data to allow it to be transmitted over the phone company's frame relay network.

frame type

A type of packet. NetWare 2.x and 3.x used the Ethernet 802.3 packet scheme; NetWare 4.x uses more-standard Ethernet 802.3 frames. The only thing you have to know about frame types in a Netware context is that you must run the same frame type on the client's network card as you're running on the server's network card so that they can communicate.

FTP

File transfer protocol, the piece of the TCP/IP protocol suite that enables users to copy files between computers.

gateway

A catchall term to describe a system that essentially bridges two systems. Gateways can pass mail, translate protocols, forward packets and perform other tasks. A gateway's primary purpose is communication.

gateway protocols

Members of the TCP/IP protocol suite that routers use to determine the best route for data packets.

groupware application

A software application that allows people to use networked computers to work together. Groupware often helps increase efficiency by automation the flow of work from person to person and reducing the overall amount of paper generated by a task.

GUI

Graphical user interface, a shell on a computer's operating system that graphically represents data. Windows, the MacOS interface and UNIX's Motif are all GUIs.

hacker

A much-misused term. A hacker does not break into computer systems (a cracker does that); instead, a hacker is a skilled programmer and problem solver. The sobriquet is seldom accurate if self-endowed.

hard drive

A nonremovable magnetic media drive that stores data.

header

The part of a packet that carries information about the source and destination of a packet, the checksum and any other data about the packet.

hexadecimal notation

Base-16 notation. In hexadecimal notation, you count from 0 to 15 like this: 0, 1, 2, 3, 4, 5, 6, 7, 8, 9, A, B, C, D, E, F.

HTML

Hypertext Markup Language, a way of formatting plain text so that it can be displayed as graphical text in a browser window. HTML uses tags, or online formatting commands, to define how things look. For example, <h1> This is a header </h1> is interpreted by a browser as a command to format the text This is a header in the header-1 style (whatever that has been defined as).

HTTP

Hypertext Transfer Protocol, the piece of the TCP/IP protocol suite used to transmit World Wide Web documents across the Internet.

hub

A colloquial term for Ethernet concentrators.

I/O or throughput

Generally, a loose measure of the speed at which a particular piece of hardware can move data. A fast processor, for example, is said to have better I/O than a slow one. I/O is most commonly applied to devices that have to actually move information; hard drives that have to send and retrieve data from the network.

IDE

Integrated Drive Electronics, a way of attaching hard drives to computers using logic built into the hard drive rather than using a third-part device.

IMAP

Interactive Mail Access Protocol, a new piece of the TCP/IP protocol suite that handles the transmission of mail between server and client. IMAP largely supplants POP; its current revision is IMAP4.

infrared

The light spectrum just shorter than red: invisible to human eyes. Infrared is often used for line-of-sight data transmission in wireless networks.

internet

The global network of networks now used for everything from email to electronic commerce to research.

interoperability

The capability of two products to operate together, ideally according to open standards such as the TCP/IP protocol.

IP

Internet Protocol the part of the TCP/IP protocol responsible for providing addressing and routing services to packets. IP ensures that packets are addressed properly.

IP address

A sequence of numbers associated with a network adapter's MAC address. It is 32 bits long and is divided into four 1-byte strings that have values ranging from 0 to 255.

IPX

Internetworking Packet Exchange, the part of Novell NetWare's IPX/SPX protocol responsible for addressing and routing.

ISDN

Integrated Services Digital Network a switched digital phone service that in its Basic Rate Interface (BRI) can carry upto 128 kilobits per second of data; in its Primary Rate Interface (PRI), it can be as fast as 1.5 megabits per second. ISDN is very useful for connecting remote users who have high-speed network requirements.

ISP

Internet service provider, a company that provides connections to the Internet. The connections can range from dial-up to from relay, depending on the ISP and connection speed desired.

Java

A programming language invented by Sun Microsystems that enables programmers to write software that can run on any platform using a Java Virtual Machine developed for that platform.

jumper

A very small piece of plastic (less than 1/8 inch on a side) with a conductive metal strip inside it. Jumpers are used (like switches) to make electrical connections on a card.

LAN

Local area network, a group of computers in a local area tied together without any routers between them. All computers connected to the same set of hubs or switches in a LAN and all network resources are "local," running at the full speed of the network.

Linux

A freeware Unix-like operating system developed by Linux Torvalds and a host of Internet programmers. Linux is free, fast and astonishingly stable. If you have to learn Unix, Linux is a great place to start.

logical segment

A network configuration in which a single network segment is simulated through the use of devices called concentrators.

login script

A text file stored on the server that has a list of commands. When a user logs in, the server reads the text file, executes the commands included in it and often maps drives and connects network printers on-the-fly for each user. Typical login scripts can include lines that don't do anything except let the user know that he or she is being logged in; the login script can also include commands such as net use which establish network connections to other computers.

MAC address

Media Access Control address, a 6-byte (48-bit) address unique to each and every network card, represented in hexadecimal notation.

MAN

Metropolitan Area Network, a group of LANs in a relatively small geographical area joined by digital phone lines or by other technologies such as microwave radio.

MAU

Multistation Access Unit, IBM's name for a Token Ring concentrator.

memory

The chips that provide a place for the computer to store the 1s and 0s it needs to do computations. Memory chips are fast – an order of magnitude faster than virtual memory.

modem

Short for modulate-demodulate. A device used to convert digital signals into analog tones that can be transmitted over the telephone network.

multitasking

In operating systems, the capability to divide computer time among two or more running programs simultaneously.

NDS

NetWare Directory Services, a set of standards for organizing enterprise networks. Proprietary to Novell, but available on many systems. Very powerful for organizing and logically segmenting networks.

NetBEUI

NetBIOS Extended User Interface, an extension of NetBIOS that includes the capability to frame packets. (NetBEUI Frame or NBF) among other extended features. NetBEUI is a common implementation of NetBIOS.

NetBIOS

Network Basic I/O System, a small, non-routable protocol developed by IBM for small PC networks.

network

Any conglomeration of parts working together in a predictable order. In computer terms, a group of computers connected by a common topology that enables data to be transmitted.

NETWORK ADAPTER

An adapter card installed in a computer that allows it to communicate on a network.

NFS

Network Interface Card, also called network adapters; an add-in card that plugs into a computer and enables it to communicate on a network. NICs are usually ATM. Ethernet (of one variety or another), Token Ring or FDDI.

NLM

NetWare Loadable Module a program that can execute natively on a NetWare server. Most NLMs can be loaded and unloaded on-the-fly. They control a great many NetWare functions, from the protocols it uses (IPX, NLM and SPX.NLM) to backup and administration (MONITOR.NLM).

NOS

Network Operating System, software that allows a computer to perform certain network-centric tasks such as authenticating users, handling file security and providing connections to network resources. Windows NT server, Unix and NetWare are NOSes.

Octet

The "official" name for a byte (eight bits, or eight digital 1s and 0s).

open standards

Hardware and software standards that are not proprietary to any given manufacturer. TCP/IP and Ethernet are both open standards.

operating system

The software on a computer that enables the user to communicate with the hardware and get tasks done. Windows 95, Windows NT Workstation, OS/2 and Unix are all operating systems.

optical fiber

The medium used by fiber-optic networks. Most networks use either coaxial cable or UTP.

OSI model

Open Systems Interconnect Model, a reference model that details seven layers of functionality for networks. The OSI model offers an ideal way to understand the theory of networking.

OSPF

Open Shortest Path First, a routing protocol that uses what's called a link-state algorithm. Link-state algorithms look at the available routers a data packet can take to its destination and decide the best route. OSPF does not have a maximum hop count as RIP does.

packet

Also called a diagram; information placed inside a "wrapper" called the header. Packet contain header (which handle addressing), error correction, checksums and (eventually) the data sent across the network.

packet header

see header.

packet-switcher

A technology in which binary data is divided into small packages that handle error collection and address information to transmit data across a physical medium such as cable.

PC card

A credit-card-seized electronic device that slides into a slots on the side of a laptop. PC cards can be almost anything, but they are usually network adapters and modems.

peer-to-peer

A network built without a central server. In a peer network, all computers can be both servers and clients as required. Generally unmanageable, but useful for small networks.

plaintext

The text of a message in human-readable format. In other words, to be or not to be in an example of a plaintext message.

Plug and Play

Adapter card hardware for which I/O addresses and IRQs are set through software rather than through hardware jumpers of some sort.

POP

Post Office Protocol, the TCP/IP standard for mail transmission between server and client. POP3 is the current version.

Porting

The process of recompiling C language source code into versions that can run on different computers.

POTS

Plain Old Telephone Service, the regular old Ma Bell dial tone used for voice and modems.

PPP

Point-to-Point Protocol, the part of the TCP/IP protocol suite used to connect computers across switched telephone lines – either regular phone service (POTS) or switched digital service (ISDN).

programming languages

Standardized ways of creating instructions for computers. Common programming languages include C, Fortran, Java, Smalltalk, COBOL, APL and others.

protocol

As agreed-on standard. In networking terms, a protocol is used to address and ensure delivery of packets across a network.

protocol translator

A device that can translate between two network protocols. Typically, protocol translators translate NetWare IPX to TCP/IP so that uses on an IPX network can access the Internet or IP resources.

proxy server

A server that hides internal network IP addresses from the Internet by making requests for the internal clients.

QoS

Quality of Service; in packet data, QoS is very similar in regular mail. In regular mail, you have a choice of services – first class, second class, third class, bulk mail, overnight and so forth. When you send an overnight letter, it receives priority over first-class mail, so it gets to its destination first. A few bits of data in a packet of data indicate the QoS required for that data. QoS is an evolving standard and will hopefully be common on all platforms and topologies within the next few years.

RAID

Redundant Array of Inexpensive Disks, a method of ensuring data security, ranging from simple disk mirroring with two disks (RAID) to stripping all data across three or more disks (RAID 5).

redundancy or fault tolerance

The capability of a computer system to shrug off the failure of a device and continue operating normally. Generally, redundant devices send a message to an administrative user when a particular device fails so that the device can be replaced. Redundancy is often implemented by simply adding a second device (a second hard drive, network card or whatever). Of late, however, IBM-compatible computers are beginning to use clustering for redundancy (when a whole extra machine is on standby, waiting for the first one to fail).

repeater

A device that enables networks to communicate reasonably well. A repeater amplifies and cleans up digital signals and forward them on towards their destination.

RIP

Routing Information Protocol, a protocol that works by counting the number of times a packet has been moved toward its destination. Each new routing is called a hop and the maximum hop count is usually set to 16. In RIP, if a packet is routed more than 16 times, it's discarded.

RMON

Remote Monitoring, the part of the TCP/IP protocol suite hat handles network management and network data collection. RMON is much more efficient than its older sibling, SNMP.

router

A device or (optionally) software that routers toward their destinations. Routers must be connected to at least two networks. They decide how to send data based on network conditions.

routing tables

A database of routes between networks that router carry in their memory. In general, the smaller the routing table, the faster the router.

RPC

Remote Procedure Call, a method used on client/server networks for communicating between processes (applications) running on different computers. RPC is sometimes used to distribute work across a network according to appropriateness. For example, a server running a database might handle searches locally, while queries are generated at the client computer.

scalable

The measure of a system's capability to grow. It is not quantifiable: unfortunately, there is no standard against which to compare a particular system. As a result, scalability is relative. For example, if a network has 10 users and grows to 100, will the current network architecture continue to work well? If the answer is yes, the system is scalable; if he answer is no, the system is not scalable.

scope creep

A process in which the scope of a job grows while the job is in process. Scope creep is the bane of projects managers; it almost guarantees that a given project will be over budget and late.

Scripting language

A limited programming language built into many operating systems.

SCSI

Small Computer Serial Interface, pronounced "scuzzy;" a method for connecting a variety of peripherals to a computer. SCSI devices include hard drives, CD-ROM drives, scanners and so on.

separate memory spaces

In Windows NT (versions 3.5x to 4.x) it is possible to run 16-bit applications (that is, older Windows applications) in their own memory space. This means that if and when these applications misbehave, they theoretically can't crash other applications.

server

A computer on a network that shares resource (file, print, applications with other computers.

share

Microsoft's method for allowing computers to access othe computers' drives and printers as though those resources were loca

shell

The interactive users interface in an operating system of networ operating system. The shell takes the user's commands either a the command line (the DOS c-prompt, for example) or through graphical user interface (the Windows interface, for example) an passes them to the operating system or network operating systerr

shell script

In Unix, a text file containing operating system commands. Whe the name of the shell script is typed as a command line, the serie of command sin the file runs. DOS has a pale shadow of she scripting called batch files. Batch files do much the same thing, bu because DSO can do only one thing at a time, batch files are c limited use.

SLIP

Serial Line Internet Protocol, an older standard, part of the TCP/I protocol suite used to connect computers over phone lines Supersded by PPP.

SMTP

Simple Mail Transmission Protocol the TCP/IP standard for interne mail. SMTP exchanges mail between servers; contrast this wit POP, which transmits mail between a server and a client.

Sneaker Net

How files got moved before networks – usually with floppy disks and a bit of shoe leather or sneaker rubber (hence the name).

SNMP

Simple Network Management Protocol, the piece of the TCP/IP protocol suite that deals with the transmission of network information for system administration and management. SNMP is not as efficient as its younger sibling, RMON.

Soft-set

See Plug and Play.

SOHO

Small Office/Home Office, a term used to describe the increasingly decentralized office market. SOHO devices typically support from one to four users instead of many users.

Source code

The text files written by programmers that are fed into compilers; the compilers output executable files that the computer can understand so that programs can run.

Star topology

A network topology in which all connections pass through a central device called a concentrator. 10BASE-T, Token Ring, FDDI and ATM all use star topologies.

Striping

The process by which a RAID device controller card writes data to multiple disks.

subnet

A way of dividing TCP/IP networks into smaller pieces fo management or security purposes. Subnets are bridged by routers

subnet mask

The portion of an IP address that defines the network, as opposed tc identifying a particular computer. For example, a computer with ar IP address of 192.168.1.5. might have a subnet mask o 255.255.255.0. The portion of the address that reads 192.168.1 is the network address and the .5 is the address of the specific machine on that network. The subnet mask explains that the first three numbers in a dotted-decimal address (for example, 192.168.1) are the network and that the last number denotes a specific compute on that network.

switching

A technology in which each connection between two computes ha a dedicated channel available to only those two computers at an given time.

T 1

A digital phone line that can carry data at speeds of up to 1.54 megabits per second.

tag

In HTML, a formatting device. A tag starts with formatting comman between two angle brackets (<HEADING 1>) and ends with the sam command preceded by a slash (<HEADING 1>).

TCP

Transmission Control Protocol, the part of the TCP/IP protocol suit that ensures reliable delivery of packets to their destinations.

TCP/IP

Transmission Control Protocol/internet Protocol, a catchall term to describe the multifaceted protocol suite on which the Internet runs. TCP/IP is also an open standard; it is not owned by or proprietary to any company. Anyone can create an implementation of the TCP/IP protocol if they want to do so.

Thinnet

Yet another colloquial name for 10BASE-2 Ethernet.

throughout or I/O

Generally, a loose measure of thė speed at which a particular piece of hardware can move data. A fast processor, for example, is said to have better throughput than a slow one. Throughput is most commonly used to describe devices that have to actually move information: hard drives that have to read and write information to and from their drive platters and network cards that have to send and retrieve data from the network.

Token Ring

A topology that exchanges data between computers by token passing rather than CSMA/CD.

topology

In networking terms, a topology is nothing more than the arrangement of a network. The term can refer to the physical layout of the network (which is where 10BASE-2, 10BASE-T and fiber come in to the arrangement) or the logical layout of the network.

transceiver

The part of the network adapter card that manages sending and receiving data packets from the network wire.

tunnelling protocol

A protocol that ensures that data passing over a company's Virtual Private Network is secure. Tunneling is similar to putting a letter/envelope addressed to a non-local company mailstop in another, larger envelope that uses postal mail to send it to another company location. When the mail gets to the nonlocal company mailstop, the mail clerks it out of the large envelope and send it on to the person to whom it's addressed.

UDP

User Datagram Protocol, the part of the TCP/IP protocol suite that handles "unreliable" delivery of packets. In other words, UDP handles the delivery of packets over links that aren't always available.

Unix

An operating system developed by Bell Labs during the late 1960s and early 1970s. Arguably the best OS for mission-critical applications because of almost 30 years of refinement. Common Unix vendors are Sun Microsystems and Santa Cruz Operation (SCO).

user group

In Windows NT domains, a class of domain users grouped together for simplified administration. Groups are created and managed in the Windows NT User Manager for Domains application. Users can have specific privileges assigned and specific resources made available as the result of their membership in a user group. For example, user group Accounting might have access to the system's accounting files and applications. Users not in the Accounting user group do not have access to those resources.

UTP

Unshielded twisted-pair wire, a cable with four pairs of wires (blue, orange, green and brown) used for Ethernet and Token Ring network wiring.

VAR

Value Added Reseller, a reseller who also handles integration and project management tasks.

virtual memory

Space on a disk dedicated to providing memory space when the capacity of physical memory chips has been exceeded.

VLAN

Virtual Local Area Network, a network established over a carrier's digital phone lines (such as AT & T or Script lines) and dedicated solely to connecting several specific client sites. Used to implement WANs by using the Internet to create a quasi-private network.

WAN

Wide area network, a network composed of two or more LANs connected by phone lines (generally digital phone lines) and routed between segments.

Windows 95

Microsoft's client operating system.

Windows NT

Microsoft's enterprise operating system. Fully premptive and reliable.

winsock

A set of files, usually centered around a file called Winsock.dll, that Windows uses to interact with TCP/IP.

WWW

World Wide Web, the resources that can be accessed on the Internet using HTTP, often published in HTML.

yellow-cable Ethernet

Another term for 10BASE-5 ("thicknet") Ethernet.

9

QUESTIONS

CHAPTER 1 — INTRODUCTION TO NETWORKING

1. What are the basics of Networking?

2. Describe the various aspects of Local Area Networking.

3. Describe the various aspects of Wide Area Networks.

4. Describe the various types of Wide Area Networks?

5. Discuss the advantages and disadvantages of

   Ring Networking

   Mesh Networking

   Bus Networking

   Star Networking

   Hybrid Networking

   Tree Networking

6. Discuss the various uses of networking.

Chapter 2 — Setting up the Cables

1. Descibe Ethernet Cables.

2. Describe the various advantages and disadvantages of Thinnet Cables.

3. Describe the process of installing conduits and Wall boxes.

4. Describe the various cables you need for networking.

5. Describe the design of twisted pairs.

6. Describe the installation of twisted pair cabling.

Chapter 3 — Designing Your Network

1. Describe the advantages of designing the network.

2. How would you decide which computer in networking will do what?

3. How would you chalk out the logical diagram of the networking?

4. How would you write the specifications of your network?

5. Describe the process of selecting hardware for networking.

Chapter 4 — Configuring Windows for Networking

1. Describe the process of the installing Microsoft Network.

2. Describe the process of installing Protocols.

3. What are names, workgroups in terms of networking?

4. How would you install File and Printer sharing?

5. How would you set various levels of security?

CHAPTER 5 — SETTING UP HARDWARE FOR INTERNET

1. What is Internet Access?

2. Describe the various aspects of ISDN?

3. Describe the various types of Mdoems?

4. How would you configure Modem into your computer?

5. Write a brief note on ISDN hardware.

CHAPTER 6 — GETTING CONNECTED TO INTERNET

1. Who are Internet Service Providers?

2. What are e-mail services?

3. How would you install Dial Up Adapter?

4. How would you connect Modem?

5. How would you share a modem?

6. What criteria would you adopt for selecting am ISP?

7. How would you use Internet Connection Wizard?

Chapter 7 — Networking Software

1. What are the advantages of NetWare networking?
2. What are the disadvantages of NetWare networking?
3. How does Windows help in networking?
4. What are the basics of Windows 2000 Server?
5. What are the features of Unix as an operating system?
6. What are concepts of Windows networking?

Titles in the Learning Series

1. Windows 98
2. Word 2000
3. Excel 2000
4. PowerPoint 2000
5. Access 2000
6. FrontPage 2000
7. Office 2000
8. PageMaker 6.5
9. Photoshop 5.5
10. CorelDRAW 9.0
11. Internet and e-mail
12. DOS 6.0/6.22
13. Outlook 2000
14. FrontPage 2000
15. Flash 4
16. JAVA
17. HTML 4
18. C++
19. Windows ME
20. JAVA Servlets
21. UNIX
22. JavaScript
23. Visual Basic 6.0
24. Tally 5.4
25. AutoCAD 2000
26. XML/XHTML
27. Flash 5.0
28. Photoshop 6.0
29. Oracle 8i
30. CorelDRAW 10
31. e-commerce
32. Word 2002
33. Excel 2002
34. Access 2002
35. PowerPoint 2002
36. FrontPage 2002
37. Microsoft Office XP
38. Computer Fundamentals
39. C#
40. C
41. Dreamweaver 4.0
42. Red Hat Linux 7.1
43. Windows XP
44. Networking

Forthcoming Titles in the Learning Series

PageMaker 7.0

Tally 6.3

Oracle 9i

Active Server Pages

PL/SQL Programming